The Ultima Facebook Ad Campaigns for Loan Officers

How to Use Social Media and Google to Generate More Leads, Build Your Network and Close More Deals

By Carl White and Chris Johnstone

FREE STRATEGY CALL

This book includes a free strategy call to identify your best social media marketing priorities and opportunities.

Get It NOW at

LoanOfficerAds.com/call

Published by
Mortgage Marketing Animals
MortgageMarketingAnimals.com

Copyright 2019 The Marketing Animals
Printed in the United States of America

Names: White, Carl, author. Johnstone, Chris, author.
Title: The Ultimate Guide to Facebook Ad Campaigns for Loan Officers
Description: First edition | Florida: The Marketing Animals, June 2019
ISBN- 978-1-7324655-3-4 (paperback)

Dedication

To our Freedom Club and Mortgage Marketing Animals Connected Members who are sharing, testing and pushing the edges of our industry.

Table of Contents

Introduction: You Are A Pioneer!

What you hold in your hands is our cumulative and hard-earned experience over many, many years that can literally change the way you do business.

There are only three ways for you to get more customers - (1) your past clients, (2) your referral partners, and (3) leads generated from marketing and advertising. Our focus is going to be on how to do all three better by leveraging technology to create an automated flow of old and new customer leads so you can achieve more income with less effort.

By the end of this book, you will have a distinct set of daily action steps to follow. All you need to do from there is show up consistently to achieve the results you want in your business.

To set the stage, here is a powerhouse quote from marketing guru Dan Kennedy:

"The most dangerous number in business is one."

You can interpret that in a few ways – but following are our thoughts.

1) It's hard to be successful without a team.

2) If you are relying on one source of customers in your business, you are allowing yourself to be at constant risk. Rate changes, industry guideline changes, or something as simple as losing your database could take your business down (and yes, we have seen it happen).

3) One of anything isn't good - one rate, one term, one loan program, one referral partner... you get the picture.

Please don't misunderstand! You absolutely should be marketing to your database and doing so in a way that enables you to harvest the maximum number of referrals and profit from it. What we are saying is that this should not be your ONLY source of business.

For this book, we will focus primarily on using marketing and advertising technology to expand your pool of potential customers.

So, who is using this technology to grow their business? Only the most visionary loan officers who 'get' the power of being a pioneer; forging new ways to gain visibility, authority and credibility in their markets. And now, that's you.

Here is what to expect in this book so you can get the most out of it.

Our intention in sharing this information is to eliminate all the confusion and frustration we see surrounding online marketing in our industry. Online marketing is incredibly powerful BUT it is not a standalone system. It is part of an overall marketing plan. Facebook, Instagram, Google and YouTube are just some of the tools you need to have a holistic marketing system.

Yes, they each can work as a standalone marketing tactic, but you can exponentially increase your results by giving yourself a proper overall marketing plan that generates results from all areas of your business. We call this Customer Lifecycle Marketing.

We will lay out the foundation for that kind of system in this book. We want you to know we understand the significance of your loan career and business. It's how you feed your family, it's your professional identity, and it's how you serve your community and business partners.

Even if you are relatively new to the business, you have customers whose lives you have enriched by helping them become a homeowner.

This information is going to help you take your career to the next level by helping you achieve more with less effort. You can leverage technology into a customized, automated flow of new customers by building relationships.

The technology is a tool; the win is the relationships you gain by having exposure to new audiences. Statistically, it only makes sense that your business will grow – more leads, more deals, more referrals – because you are working with more relationships.

What you learn here will obviously only work when you put it into action. Carl is a no-nonsense kinda guy – he doesn't blow smoke or tell you it's easy. Chris likes to accelerate results with technology, but this is NOT a get-rich-quick scheme. Be prepared to act on what you read here. We got your back if you need support – no worries! But your results - based on what you learn here - are solely up to you.

We wrote this book to give you value, show you what's working today and start a conversation. We want you to get to know us and we want to get to know you. Ultimately, we may work together someday. If that happens, great! No matter what, we are here to help you compress the time between where you are and where you want to be in your business.

In our industry, technology can be a blocker... and you can't afford for that to be the case anymore. Be ready to stretch and consider new possibilities for you and your business.

Are we going to invite you to do more? Absolutely! We want you to have what you want – more leads, more deals, more referrals. And we want you to be smart about where you allocate your advertising dollars to do it. So, you'll see bonus materials and, yes, we do have some great training you can invest in to continue your new direct marketing ads education. Your success is our passion, so we have different ways to help you depending on your goals and resources.

Having said that, if you like what you read (or most of it), we want to hear from you. We want to get to know you better so please post a success story, picture, video and/or comment on our Facebook wall at Facebook.com/MortgageMarketingAnimals.

It is our privilege to share what you're about to read for using direct response online advertising to generate more leads, build your network and close more deals so you can be more awesome and experience greater freedom every day. We take your time and investment in this book seriously and know it can pay off for you.

Let's get started.

Sincerely,

Carl White and Chris Johnstone

Why Should You Listen to Us?

When it comes to technology, there's always something new. It seems every ten minutes brings a new app (application) or new feature or new whiz-bang something or other that you need to have to be successful. How do you know you need that whiz-bang gizmo? Should you listen to the kid behind the curtain - the self-proclaimed expert who graduated high school last year - who knows how to use digital technology to market himself or herself as an authority persona? Who DO you trust when it comes to technology?

We're not knocking anybody's ambition, talent or ability to market well - that's not the point. The point is there are a lot of so-called "experts" and it can be really confusing to know who to listen to, know what you really need and how to use it for your own business.

Many loan officers get stuck when it comes to thinking about online direct response ads and digital campaigns. Maybe they don't think they are tech-savvy enough or they get overwhelmed with ideas or where to start... maybe they don't see anybody else doing it (which is really an advantage!) or they don't know what to look for in hiring someone reputable to help them. That's why we decided to write this book together.

If you have been around Carl for any length of time, you know he is a fan of technology and a closet nerd. He has videos and audios and webinars and a solid social media presence. He's been a trailblazer in the industry and is the 'godfather' of creative marketing strategies for loan officers since his beginning in the industry. (He doesn't have enough fingers and toes to count that far back...)

Being the visionary he is, Carl knows a good opportunity when he sees it. Online marketing has been good to him. If he doesn't know what he needs to know, he goes out and learns it and/or hires the expertise he needs to make it work for him. In doing that, he's learned a lot. And he's a giver... his intention is for every loan officer to experience the kind of success he's enjoyed in his career.

As for Chris, he is one of those naturally techie-types who just 'got' the power of leveraging technology to reach people. He can get as detailed as you want when it comes to analytics but he's also a master teacher of practical strategies. He knows business has gone digital and those who can't use it risk being left behind. He can speak both digital AND business, with more than a decade of success to prove it. His company has continued to grow year-over-year since he started it. He grew up in the industry (his father is a mortgage originator) and is committed to helping loan officers make the most of direct response advertising for their business growth.

So, what do you choose? To work with a couple of guys who have seen it, learned it the hard way and proven what works with experience over years… or miss the opportunity that could be the make-or-break factor for your business today?

Assuming you want to keep reading, that's what you'll find here – real-world, leading-edge strategies, examples, scripts and ideas on how to work with social marketing campaigns that work when you apply them.

Here's to using direct online response advertising and leveraging social technology to generate more leads, build your network and close more deals!

Know Your Baselines

Let's start at the beginning. Where do you get most of your customers today? Go through your past 10-15 transactions to see where they came from as your answer to that question can be illuminating.

If you've been in the business for more than four years, there is a very high chance you answered that question with "referrals from past customers" or "referrals from business partners."

In the following chapters, we are going to give you three campaigns that can help you generate even more referrals from your past client database and your referral partners. (We'll even help you meet new referral partners.)

But we are not stopping there! We are also going to help you analyze your business and make sure you are generating as much profit as possible.

Your Average Commission Per Deal

Let's begin by calculating your average commission per deal. Why? Because you need to know this number to project your results. Online advertising is a strategy for which you need to know your ROI (return on investment). It will help form your strategy for the amount of online advertising you want to do over time.

To calculate your average commission per loan, take your income and divide it by the number of loans you closed last year. This number will help determine how many additional deals you need to do this year to achieve your goal.

For example, if your goal is to triple your business, you will know how many deals you must create with this strategy to hit that goal. Then it becomes very easy to map out - here's how many deals I need to create, here's the actions I need to take in each of these three areas of my business in order to make that happen, and then here's the easiest way to go about doing that.

You want to be able to answer this question: What's going to take the least amount of effort to get the most return in order to hit that number?

Off-Line Closing Expectation Ratios

While we're at it, let's talk about our experience with closing ratios so you know what to reasonably expect for results. (When we say "off-line," we mean relationship marketing in the real world.)

From your closed client database (DB) combined with your 'warm' network (also called your Sphere of Influence, or SOI), you should be closing two deals a month per 100 contacts. Your warm network includes your friends, family, coworkers, college buddies, business acquaintances (CPA, financial planner, attorneys, business leads group members, etc.), fellow soccer parents, church friends and others. You should be marketing to these groups consistently.

That means if you have 300 people in your DB/SOI, you should be closing six deals a month (every month) as a baseline from the marketing you're sending to that database. If you're not, this book is going to be transformational for you because it will get you to at least that as a baseline, and likely much more.

In terms of referral partners, Carl likes to qualify and classify them in three levels - whales, tunas, and tilapias. It might sound a little weird but it's brilliant. (That statement might even be a description of Carl in general - a little weird but brilliant!)

Here's what it means... if you work with a whale of a Realtor®, they can send you a lot more business than someone who is potentially doing three or four transactions a year. (This level of business is what we call guppies because they are, hopefully, working toward generating more business.)

A whale, by our definition, closes 36 or more buyer side transactions a year. A tuna closes 12-35 buyer sides a year, while a tilapia closes 8-11 deals per year. So, when you get a yes from a qualified Realtor partner and apply what you will be learning in this book, each of those new relationships should be worth at least six deals per year to you.

Now you can average that out for your business. For every individual Realtor referral partner you get in your network, that relationship will turn into an additional six deals per year. (Be sure to focus on whales and tunas for the fastest results.)

Online Closing Ratios

Now on to digital marketing closing ratios – this means Google and social media channels.

For every 100 leads you generate through Google, you should have about a 10% closing ratio. That means when someone finds you on Google, goes through your marketing system and submits an application, every 100 leads generated from Google should yield 10 closings.

On social media channels, like Facebook, Instagram and YouTube, your closing ratio should be about 4%. That means for every 100 leads you generate on social channels, you should have about four deals in your pipeline.

Now you've got a baseline of right expectations of what's going to come from each loan source. That means you are ready to go through this book and map out how much business you're going to get from these lead sources.

First, plan where you want to go in your business and how many deals you want to have from each of lead generation source. From there, every day when you go into your business, you know you've got to work the 'critical inch' by doing three things: 1) work your past clients, 2) work your referral partners, and, 3) work your marketing and advertising plan. It becomes simple and, yes, even fun to use your plan to achieve your future income goals.

Secret Sauce: Compounding Experience

When someone does business with you, are you actively creating a relationship with that person? Meaning, when they leave your office, are you memorable? Are you just processing their loan or are you creating an experience? Because there is a dramatic difference between providing a service and providing an experience.

Research shows that 95% of purchase decisions are made in the subconscious mind. We all like to think "marketing" doesn't work on us, like we're super-human and immune to it, but that's simply not true. After all, loan officers are human too, right?

When marketing a product or service to a potential consumer, experts say it's most effective to target the subconscious mind. That's an odd concept because we are actively, shamelessly and upfront marketing to these people using the power of repetition. So, it's not very subconscious. And yet, when you do it right, you are activating the subconscious mind to support making a buying decision.

We've discovered there are five drivers your clients need to experience to become an advocate of your business. This is not just about getting a good review on social media but about extending their experience by telling their friends and people in their circles about you and your memorable, positive experience. Essentially, delivering an exceptional customer experience (CX) compounds your return on effort because your customers will do your marketing for you.

Two Stages and Five Drivers of CX

There are two stages to working with a customer experience orientation – the front-end and the backend. You need six to eight marketing touches to bring people in as a customer on the front-end, and then you need six to eight different marketing touches on the backend to convert them into being a long-term advocate and brand ambassador for your business.

Here are the five key drivers that help progress the customer experience with you through any deal:
1) the actual experience your customer has with your brand before and during the loan process,
2) understanding and articulating your customer's relationship with you,

3) setting expectations for what will happen post-transaction,

4) asking for referrals with a systematic process in place, and,

5) maintaining consistent awareness and a positive feedback loop.

The first driver is the actual experience they have with you while in the transaction, created by how you are on the phone, how your staff handles their inquiries and visits, the quality of your emails, etc. This most fundamental level of experience and is comprised of all the details that create a feeling around how you do business. If it's just the basic, regular standard treatment, you'll do okay. But if it's *exceptional*, you'll create a bond with your customers which will make it much easier to get referrals from them later.

By going through the process of doing business with you, they're going to know, like and trust you - that's just the standard. You tell them what you're going to do. You do it, and then you go a little bit above and beyond on the delivery of the service. Unfortunately, in today's service economy, that's often enough to create a phenomenal customer experience because there are so many negative brand experiences out there.

Next, you have to understand and clearly articulate your customer's relationship with you. It's a good idea to clarify upfront what will happen after the deal is done when in the beginning of your relationship. This makes sure you avoid surprises when it comes to asking for a review later.

You can set expectations by saying something like, "*Here is what is going to happen...once we get a great loan that's comfortable for your lifestyle and budget, and close on your new home, can we agree that experience will be worth a five-star review online?*" Naturally, the client says "*Yes.*"

At the end of the transaction, many loan officers expect referrals without ever clearly articulating to the customer they are in the business of referrals! You must set that expectation with your customer before their loan closes for a smooth referral process later.

Additionally, you'll need a process in place to get those referrals. You need to have a phone number they can dial to leave a verbal referral, or ask them to send an email referral to a specific email address, or tell them how to tag you in a social media post and/or comment or how to make an effective personal introduction. You must clearly articulate the best process to make referrals happen. We are, by nature, repetitive as human beings. We want a process to follow, so you make referrals more natural for your customer(s) by having a process in place.

Remind your clients they gain social status by being a connector - the person who helps their friends by referring you as an exceptional experience provider and business professional.

Post-closing, you also need to create consistent brand awareness with your customer for six to eight touches, while providing a positive feedback loop. When people achieve success, they want to share it and they can't tell their success story without sharing who helped them along the way – that would be you. Give your customer the language to use, share how your other customers have told their stories about you and make sure they know how to tell their story.

PRO TIP: When somebody sends you a referral, do something nice for them (as long as it is RESPA-compliant, which means confirms to the Real Estate

Settlement Procedures Act). Reach out, give them a gift card, a love note or some other expression of gratitude for them thinking of you for a referral. Be a class act.

You want to compound your customer's experience with all good things. Essentially, that means you deliver next-level exceptional experience. Bonus - you can do that by adding different touch points to your automated marketing systems too. We'll get to that later.

Three Campaigns for Past Clients

What happens after the loan closes? How did your client feel about you, your staff, your process?

Once a loan closes, there is no recurring revenue and no real reason for your client to stay in contact with you. Yes, there is a lifetime customer value for you but, more immediately, you are going to fall into one of two 'buckets' post-close for your client. In fact, when your clients move into their new house, and they are surrounded by moving boxes and everybody is eating pizza, they have already placed you mentally into one of two categories.

The first category is the "*Yay, we're closed! Let's get on with life.*" If this is where they place you, you're nothing but a distant memory. They're not going to remember you, much less refer you and, most likely, when they need their next loan, they will use whoever is handy at the moment. They will not become an evergreen, renewable source of income for you.

The second category is the *"OMG! That was so amazing! I can't wait to tell all my friends about what just happened to me!"* This happens when they had such a phenomenal experience with you that they will go out and talk about how amazing it was to do business with you. Basically, your customer becomes your brand advocate.

The way you can facilitate being in the second category is through brand promise consistency and having a business referral process in place.

Post-Closing Email

If you're not already doing this, our recommendation is you have an email ready to go for every new customer as soon as the loan closes. You could wait a couple of days because moving day is obviously a little hectic – the timing is not as important as the message.

The goal of the message is to celebrate their win and remind them of their previous commitment about being a reference for you. The message could be something like, "*Hope all is well with you and your family and the move is going smoothly. I know you're busy, but would you be able to do me a quick favor by taking just a couple of minutes to share your experience by leaving a testimonial? Your testimonials and referrals help me grow my business and are greatly appreciated. Over the next five days, we're testing the results of getting five-star reviews on our Google My Business page. So, your help is greatly appreciated!"*

We recommend Google My Business as the place to build testimonials at first as it will provide the greatest initial return on investment, until you dominate in that space. Then you can direct people to other testimonial outlets.

Here's another example of a follow-up message which you could send the day before closing.

"Hi [borrower name]! Can I ask you a huge favor? Before you get too busy unpacking, will you take two minutes today to leave me and my team a five-star rating and a quick review? Here's the link you need, along with a quick sample layout to save you some time." Naturally, you will have examples for them.

One of your examples might be, *"We love our new home and the team that helped make it possible! We highly recommend our mortgage guru [insert your name here] to all our close friends and family."* In this example, you are embedding the expectation of referrals into the first follow-up piece that happens after the transaction.

Going further, your message could then say something like, *"We really appreciate your endorsement. While I'm asking for favors, I have another. Do you know anyone else who might be looking to buy, sell or refinance? If so, can I count on you to pass along my information? Please make sure your friends mention your name when they call. I really appreciate it."* Then include your signature with all your contact information.

You have just given them a crystal-clear pathway to follow for giving referrals. By saying "*Please make sure your friends mention your name when they call,*" you've embedded something in their subconscious we all crave - the need for significance and recognition.

Past Client Campaign #1: Lumpy Mail

After the email, we recommend sending a direct mail piece – or what we call 'lumpy mail'. This doesn't have to be fancy... just a simple token so your past customers understand you took the time to think of them and stay in touch.

Sending your customer a piece of lumpy mail is a next-level marketing strategy very few people do. It makes you seem much larger and much more professional than any of your competitors who they could have potentially done business with, it sets you up to be unforgettable in their mind, and they get a tangible thank you gift which activates the universal Law of Reciprocity where the recipient will want to give back by being an advocate for you.

The purpose of the monthly lumpy mailer is to build a long-term bond with your customer, so they keep you top of mind. You will get referrals when you mail consistently to your database but that is not the main purpose. The main goal is to make sure that your customer is willing and prepared to refer business to you every time they get the opportunity.

Consistent Awareness and Positive Feedback Loop

We've got one more driver to explore here - the consistent awareness and positive feedback loop.

One element of this strategy is to send a monthly or quarterly gift to each contact in your database. The people who go to the trouble of sending gifts to their customers typically gets more referrals. It is one of the most profitable investments to make in business because you become a talked-about subject in their life. It's unusual for people to feel appreciated for their business anymore. This is one of those small/big things that can make a huge difference in your business.

There is a service called sendoutcards.com where you can upload your database, choose a gift (like brownies) and their system will ship it out with a thank you card. You might choose to do this in-house too. Whatever way you choose to create consistent awareness through gifting, the most important thing is that you do it.

Past Client Campaign #2: Quarterly Calls

This is a simple, straightforward strategy to create consistent awareness – be the Advisor. Call every past customer in your database four times annually, which could be a lot if you have a large database. In that case, you would literally be on the phone for days, calling your past customers. That's exactly why so few people do it and it's why they lose this revenue source in their business.

By calling personally, you're renewing your bond and nurturing your connection. The initial post-close email and the lumpy mail jump-started the process, but you need six to eight touchpoints to solidify your post-close relationship. These personal follow-up calls are the next level in reaping the reward of the relationship you've built and ensuring customer retention.

There is a way to completely automate this process so it takes about 20 minutes to call your entire database, regardless of size. The key is having a script for the actual call that sets you apart from competitors or anyone your clients have 'shopped' prior to working with you.

Your calls are all likely going to go to voicemail. You're not actually going to talk to anybody live on the phone or, at least, it's unlikely that you will catch them. (By the way, if you have any call reluctance issues, please check out Carl's bestselling book called *Crushing Call Reluctance for Loan Officers.*)

Following is a script you can use to leave a voicemail.

"Hey, it's Carl White. Your name popped into my head, so I thought I'd reach out and say thanks again for your business. Lately there's been some news about mortgage rates - I wanted you to know you're still in the right product.

If anything changes about that, me or my team will let you know. Your needs are still a priority. While I'm calling, my business is built on referrals so if you know anyone who has questions about financing, refinancing or looking to buy or sell, I'd appreciate an introduction. You can send an email and copy us both, tag me on social media or pass along my number. I would love to help your friends and family have a great experience too. For now, have a great day! Thanks."

The most important part of that whole message is, "*If anything changes about that, me or my team will let you know,*" When you go back to your past customer to say, "*Hey, I'm thinking about you and I've got your back,*" it makes them feel more comfortable about all they hear in the news and continues to add value to your relationship.

Don't worry if it's been awhile since you talked with them. They aren't sitting by the phone wondering why you haven't called - simply remind them who you are and why you care. Obviously if they're no longer in the right product, you'll take that opportunity to help them accordingly.

The average person doesn't understand the real estate market, interest rates and what it all really means to their situation, which results in an uneasy feeling for them when they hear things on the news. When they know you are taking care of them even after their loan has closed, you strengthen your connection. Your customer continues to have the extra-special experience they got already, and it gives them more to rave about with their friends.

Ringless Voicemail Software

If you were wondering how you can call all the people in your DB/SOI regularly, we've got a solution for you. You can use an automated software or service like Slybroadcast or, even better, AgentLegendLO.com. Check it out and you'll see what we mean.

To use software like this, you simply upload your database, then record (and save) a voicemail you want to send in a phone message, then click "broadcast." It's just that easy. Once you do it a couple of times, it will only take about ten minutes to leave voicemail messages for everyone in your database and sphere of influence.

For the recipient, the phone call appears as a "missed" call. When they hear that nice message from you, they feel like the special people they are, reaffirming they are in the loop with you, keeping you top of mind so they can send you referrals.

If you don't want to mess with software, just work the phone yourself – chunk your call list down to what you can do in an hour and make calls until you're done. It's the investment that will pay you back.

But, to be clear, our goal is to get maximum result (profit) from the minimum amount of effort necessary. Work smarter, not harder, so leverage technology where it makes sense in your business. An automated lead conversion system means sending leads a ringless voicemail, text messages, and emails, then converting that lead into an inbound phone call.

Past Client Strategy #3: Become a Social Celebrity

Let's jump right in to our third and final strategy for past client marketing. This is a social strategy and powerful method to generate a steady stream of referrals with your past customers. In short, it's for you to become a social media celebrity.

This strategy works by leveraging the ability of Facebook (which includes Instagram) and Google Ads (which includes YouTube) to target your past customers and then 'drip' (or consistently share) valuable content where your past customers can easily see it. When they see your content, your customer will click on the call to action, engage with you on social media with comments and/or messages, and now your name is top of mind so they remember to send referrals your way. This is called Retargeting using Custom Audiences, which is a way to tell the social media channel who you want to see your ads. In this case, your Custom Audience would be your past customers.

However, while we're suggesting past clients here, remember this also works with lists of website visitors, people who engage with your content on social media, your new leads, your referral partners, etc.

Keep in mind any content you create on social media – whether a blog post, a video or an event - can be boosted with an advertisement. When you boost content with an ad, you can choose the audience you want to see it – and that audience should, in this case, be your past customers.

Some great content that provides social proof is sharing client testimonials and success stories – and these are two different things.

Testimonials

You can get testimonials directly on your social media sites, but it is probably easier to cut-and-paste one from your Google My Business page or other social media channels, or maybe from your website or what your customers shared in an email to you.

A testimonial might say something like, "*Carl was a blessing to work with. He was thorough and patient when explaining the home-buying process, which was important as we were first-time buyers and had lots of questions.*" Ideally, you'll include the person's headshot and, ideally, city and state to prove they are a real person. Make sure you have their permission to share their testimonial before posting it, if they sent it to you in an email.

This reinforces with your client that other people are having a phenomenal experience with your business so they can feel comfortable sending their friends, family members and coworkers to you since they're going to have an excellent experience. It demonstrates their personal exceptional experience with you wasn't an anomaly. Social proof gets business for you by generating referrals.

Success Stories

A success story is you, or your client, telling the story of how you helped them. These stories usually include a beginning (here's the situation), middle (what we did), and end (what happened as a result of what we did). These can be transformational because you can create a message around a specific type of customer or loan scenario you want to attract for your business.

For example, if you're going after first-time home buyers, your success story might be, "*I had a client in our office last week. They were first-time home buyers, and they didn't think that they could qualify with the down payment they had. Here's what happened,*" and then you talk about the first-time home buyer program you introduced them to, and the government grant they qualified for that they didn't know was available, and then the coaching you helped give their family about gifted down payments. You tell the story, but the subliminal message behind that story is, "*I work with first-time home buyers. There is a program for this, there's a program for this, there's a program for this. Call me if this is your scenario.*"

What happens is your past customers will read those stories and think of people they know who are in similar situations - like that first-time home buyer, or someone who is self-employed, or someone who may need a reverse mortgage (like their friends' parents). You tell the story of that transformation, and your past customers will tag their friends who are good leads for that part of your business.

Social Call to Action

Once you have your testimonial or success story in your social media channels, you share them through ads. The videos, testimonials or success stories will rotate sequentially, with one of every three showing a call to action (which means the person does something to learn more about how you can help them). We also call this the 'activator', or Referral Attractor, campaign.

This call to action is the exact same call to action that's in the post-close email, in the lumpy mail, in the voicemail... it all culminates in your past customers seeing this advertisement on their social media.

It says, "*Do you know somebody looking to buy, sell, or refinance their home? Tag them in a comment below, and* we'll make sure they get the same exceptional five-star service that all our clients get," and, at the bottom, it says, "*Thank you for your referrals.*" People see this pop up on their newsfeed so they can easily tag their friends, their family, and their coworkers in the actual social media post.

That means, as you're sitting at your desk, you will hear a 'ding!' that signals the name of somebody who's been referred into your business and who is pre-sold by one of your past customers.

Make sure you reply to the comments with something like, "*Hey, Bob. I see that Mary just referred you over my way. Here's my phone number - please give me a call.*" Then 'Bob' gives you a call, and it's just a nice, smooth referral process. It's the same as a word of mouth referral, but now you're able to create a viral effect with it for exponential numbers of referrals because you're using a little bit of advertising on an audience that's been properly pre-framed to send you all their referrals.

We've all heard of someone who goes to the local football game or the mom's group or community volunteer project, where they meet a friend and hear, "*Hey, we're buying our first house.*" And then, "*That's great! I'll refer you over to my mortgage lender.*" But what happens after they leave the party? They totally forget, they don't have your contact information, or life just happens, and it never actually makes it to you.

Your post on social media takes care of that because, a few days later, your ad pops into their newsfeed and they remember, "*Oh, yeah, I was going to refer so and so...*" It takes 10 seconds for them to tag their friend(s) in a comment on your advertisement and now you're easily getting those referrals.

Let's talk about the four types of ads next.

Four Types of Online Ads

First, you will need to set up a custom audience in your social media channel(s) with your database of past clients and centers of influence (more on how to set up a custom audience later). Then you will set up four different types of ads to be rotated to this audience over time.

Set your budget(s) very low (like, $5 per day per ad network) so the platform rotates your ads, meaning you don't bombard your past clients every time they login. Your goal is for them to see you every so often to stay top of mind without harassing them.

There are a couple of campaign metrics you want to check on weekly in Facebook - 1) your frequency score and 2) your quality score.

Frequency is how often people see your ads. Your quality score is made up of a few factors that, basically, measure whether people like your ads. Any score less than six is bad; in that case, check your frequency and write new ads.

Following are the four ad campaign types.

ONE: Success stories, testimonials and reviews from existing customers to remind your audience how awesome you are as a professional.

TWO: Education that solves your ideal client's problems or answers common questions. You can use videos, a link to online tools (like a free mortgage calculator), or even great blog posts on your website.

The point is to establish yourself as a knowledgeable professional, so people feel comfortable referring you and have a resource to use in introducing you to their network of people.

THREE: Social awareness that lets people know how you pay it forward in your community. For example, you may offer a certain percentage of every deal to a local women's shelter, work with heroes or sponsor a local Little League team.

FOUR: The final and most important campaign is the Referral Attractor, with the 'activator', or call to action.

THE REFERRAL ATTRACTOR!

- Education.

- Testimonials.

- Stories of success.

- The activator!

The text of the Referral Attractor ("activator") ad says ...

"*Do you know someone looking to buy, sell or refinance their home? Tag them in a comment below and we will make sure they get the same exceptional 5-star service all our clients get!*"

In the headline and description, put your name, phone number, email and website address.

For the ads where you have room, add a tagline like, "*Our business runs on referrals. Send us your friends, family and co-workers and we will ensure they get the same excellent service you received.*"

PRO TIP: If you want to get super fancy, you could add your Referral Activator messaging as your email signature on all emails you send out. Be sure to include a link to a page on your website that has a form where people can read your reviews and send you referrals.

To get started setting up your ads on Facebook and Instagram, go to facebook.com/business/ads.

To get started setting up your ads on YouTube and Google, go to ads.google.com.

Once you set this up the first time, you have an exceptional asset for your business that will produce referrals (and closings) for years to come.

Imagine all your past clients seeing your branding across Facebook, Instagram, YouTube and Google's content network. It's powerful to have that kind of digital presence. It's what we call Omni Channel Marketing.

THE DIGITAL MORTGAGE PROCESS

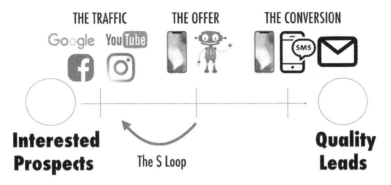

Interested Prospects

The $ Loop

Quality Leads

Act Like Your Referrals

The number one source of business is your past client database, which we just covered. Now it's time to talk about the #2 source of loans in your business today (and which many loan officers do not know this!).

Usually loan officers have no idea how to determine their sources of loans because they're not tracking the numbers. As much as we know networking works - getting face-to-face with potential Realtor partners, insurance partners and financial planners who can send you business – loan officers neglect to consider their return on investment. Your time is your most valuable asset - you want to know where it's paying off so you can focus on that and let go of what's not working.

However, if you're not tracking your results, you're probably seeing the Pareto Principle in action where 80% of your results are coming from just 20% of your efforts. That means you could be doing 80% less networking and still get the same (or better) results.

Remember our goal here is to set up automated leads from online marketing systems but also to make sure you are making the most amount of money with the least amount of effort. We wouldn't be doing our jobs if we didn't give you a bigger picture of success and direction on how to achieve it.

Honestly, if you did the above steps for each of the three past client campaigns, as well as the rest of the awesomeness you are about to get here, you could be set for the rest of your career.

To really land the power of what it means to act like your referrals, pull out your smartphone right now and do what every person does when they are given your name as a referral...

Google your name.

Do the reviews for your mortgage business show up front and center? Is it overwhelmingly clear that they should be doing business with you and no one else?

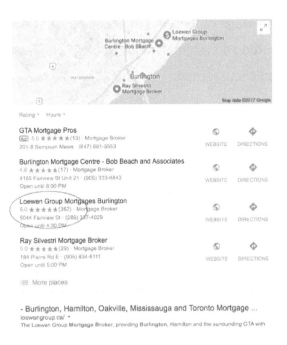

If you are not getting that kind of visibility from Google, you are losing the business your referral partners are trying to send you.

It really is that simple... just think about how you spend your own money. When you book travel, buy a car, eat at a restaurant or even make a small purchase on Amazon, how do you buy? You check the reviews. Your potential and referred customers are doing the same thing.

To take advantage of this kind of social proof, you need to focus on putting a system in place to get 5-star reviews from your past customers.

These reviews are not on your website or gathered by some third-party tool that just posts them online. Instead, you need to direct your clients to leave reviews directly on your Google My Business Page. Then on your Yelp page, and then your Facebook page - in that order.

Four Core Business Systems

At this point, you have four core business systems set up to drive more referrals and closed loans for you as soon as they are running.

1. Monthly lumpy mail to drive referrals and build your connection / referral bond.

2. Quarterly automated phone calls to your warm network.

3. Facebook, Instagram, YouTube and Google Retargeting Ads that identify your past clients for social ads and drive viral referrals over time.

4. Online 5-star reviews that drive referrals and bring in the highest-quality new leads from online platforms.

Now it's time to bring more referral partners into your business.

Networking for Referral Partners

Working with referral partners requires a plan. We've all done it... we've established a referral relationship and then, about 90 days later, discovered it wasn't a good match. It's ideal to know what you want upfront so you can focus on getting maximum results with minimum effort.

You want to find partners (yes, partners!) who are really going to help you grow and scale your business - not ones who take your time, complain, demand you work 24/7, and not send enough deals. Is this being picky? Yep. But we want you to be successful. It is absolutely okay for you to be selective in your partners. In fact, your business demands it because there's only so much time in a business day. Being selective with whom you work is a next-level business growth strategy. For your partners, you - and the results you bring - are the prize!

Your goal is to attract quality referral partners and drive more transactions for both businesses. These are win-win strategic partnerships.

Following is an outline of the total process of networking for referral partners online.

1. Identify the Realtors in your local market who actually have business to send you. Generally speaking, you want them to be able to send you enough referrals so you can close a minimum of six deals per year per referral partner.

2. Create a complete list of all these Realtors with name, email, phone number, etc.

3. Once a week - for a total of 12 weeks - reach out and ask if there is any way you can help them. If there are any changes in the market, or you have valuable tools to share with them, send those along to demonstrate your willingness to partner and provide value.

4. Set up a custom audience of Realtors on Facebook and Google, then start showing your ads to your new potential referral partners. (More on how to create a customer audience later in this book.)

Your online ads should focus on:
- Customer success stories.
- Your commitment to closing on time and customer satisfaction.
- Showcasing your personality and highlighting how much fun it is to work with you.

The main purpose of your personal calls and online ads is to support your Realtor referral partners in their business while building rapport and familiarity. When they respond to your good heartedness, you ask for a meeting.

Most importantly, do NOT talk about your business, loan products, etc. Instead, simply get to know them and build a relationship. The deals will come naturally as a result of the know, like and trust factor. It might sound simplistic but that's because it is – it's about building relationships before working together to later help each other close transactions. Leonardo da Vinci said, "*Simplicity is the ultimate sophistication.*" And we agree.

Relationships are the key to successful business. Simply follow these steps with consistency. Remember it normally takes 7 to 10 touches before you start getting referrals.

If you are in an incredibly competitive market, we have three advanced strategies for you to add to your toolkit. Each strategy has been responsible for creating a consistent flow of top-performing Realtors working with our clients. Choose the one that resonates best with you, implement it, then reach out and share your results with us!

Before we get to those strategies, let's cover how to create a Custom Audience in Facebook.

Creating a Custom Audience in Facebook

We might be getting a little ahead of ourselves but, just so you know how easy it is to create a Custom Audience in Facebook, let's go for it. In this example, we will be uploading our past database.

First, you will need a business page. Currently, you cannot do this with your personal page. Next, from your CRM system or LOS, export your database of past customers into a CSV file (which is a kind of file format). All you need is their first name, email address and phone number.

Now, go into the Ads Manager and under "Assets", click on "Audiences." You will see a big blue button that says, "Create a custom audience" - click that.

Next the system will ask you what your source will be - your answer is, "*Customer file.*"

Then Facebook will ask you to upload and name the file. You can call it Past Customers or Past Clients - whatever you'd like to call it.

And there you have your custom audience! It will take about 20 minutes for Facebook to go out and find those people on Facebook and put them into an audience for you.

Once your custom audience has been created, click on the "Create ad" button. Assuming you created ads from your testimonials, success stories and videos, you follow the steps to upload those ads, which will then target your custom audience. This is called retargeting – where people see ads based on their previous preferences and behavior.

As an example from one of our members, following is a direct message that came into our customer's business as a result of an ad run in one of their customers' newsfeeds. Their customer saw their ad, then referred a potential customer who said, "*Hi, can you help with a refinance? I own a home, but it needs repairs, and I'm not sure if refinancing is the way. Can you offer help with that?*"

After a conversational thread of about 40 messages back and forth, our (student) customer was able to convert that lead through Facebook Messenger from a referral that came from a past customer. This strategy really does work.

A key point is to make sure you close the loop on any referrals you get. When someone sends you a referral and you don't close the loop on the backend with some acknowledgement, they won't loop you into the next referral. They will send you only that first referral and, if you drop the ball on it, you leave all the rest of the money on the table.

Your acknowledgement doesn't have to be a Starbucks gift card — it can be as unassuming as a personal thank you note. Just make sure you acknowledge this person thought of you and they were the catalyst in helping someone else get what they needed. Just be cool — say thank you.

Now that we got that out of the way, following are three advanced strategies to working with more Realtor referral partners.

1. The Irresistible Offer
2. The Results in Advance Framework
3. Leveraging Listings into Leads

1. The Irresistible Offer

If you have been working to attract Realtors for any amount of time, you have already heard all their excuses and justifications for why they shouldn't work with you. "*I have been sending business to mortgage guy X for 10 years and just work with him.*" "*My people come to me already approved.*" The list goes on...

Please realize these agents are not saying no to you forever. They are just saying "*no, not right now*" and they are saying it specifically to your offer.

However, when you have the right offer for your Realtors, and you can solve a unique and expensive problem they have, your ability to attract top-performing Realtor referral partners escalates.

THE RESULTS

There is one thing you can say that is an Irresistible Offer to potential Realtor referral partners to absolutely get their attention and neutralize any objection they may have in working with you for any reason. Here it is:

"Do NOT send me your business. I just want help in closing the business I bring to you."

When you position your offer this way, you're letting that potential Realtor partner know you're not trying to get in the way of any other referral relationships they (or you) have, and you aren't trying to get them to do something that's not compliant. Chances are they will be open to hearing more from you – and that's your in. That's when you present your value proposition, whatever it is. We'll give you a few ideas about that in a bit.

In the meantime, know you are a rainmaker and a problem-solver - not an assistant - who will help bring in business.

2. The Results in Advance Framework

This campaign strategy works by completely transforming the perceived relationship between you and the Realtor referral professional by showing your value to Realtors in your market, so they chase you vs. you pursuing them.

Essentially, you will run ads on Facebook and Instagram to attract the Realtor and then give them another very specific offer. The offer is "*We have buyers who need to find a house and we need more real estate professionals to help with our leads.*"

PRO TIP: This framework also works to attract insurance agents, financial planners, title companies, etc.

By promising results in advance, you become a path to cash for your Realtor referral partners. It reduces the risk for your potential partner to consider working with you because you are bold enough to state what you can do for them upfront.

Following is a sample ad.

Keep in mind your Realtors are very easy to target on Facebook and Instagram, and this is a very compelling offer for someone looking to grow their business. Once they see this ad, they click on it and are taken to the first step in the qualification process - the opt-in page.

An opt-in page is seeking to do one thing – get the visitor to 'opt in' to a mailing list or marketing system. Following is an example of an opt-in page.

This page converts at around 20% to 25% (clicks to leads). You can build a landing page like this by using a tool like leadpages.net or clickfunnels.com.

Once the Realtor clicks on the button, they see a pop-up that asks for their contact details and to book a free 15-minute call. After they put in their contact details guess what they see… a hurdle!

Why would you want that Realtor to have to jump over hurdles to have a call with you? Because this helps you know they are serious – they're not tire-kickers but, instead, are people willing to take fast action.

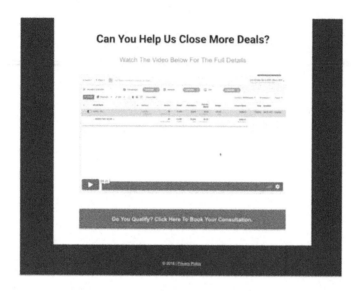

The 'hurdle', in this case, is a thank you page with a video on it, which is there just to qualify the Realtor lead again and make sure only high-producing Realtors are making it into your marketing system.

There are four key things you want to highlight in your 'hurdle' video:

1. You are showing them in advance that you are driving results in your business and that working with you is an opportunity.

2. You are telling them how much business they must be doing each month to qualify working with you.

3. You are setting a standard of service you expect them to adhere to when they are following up on your leads.

4. They are seeing you know how to turn online marketing into customers by putting them through a marketing funnel.

The start of the video kicks off by showing the results you are driving for other partners in your marketplace. This can be the leads you are converting for other Realtor partners using The Irresistible Offer OR it can be your Facebook account showing the pre-qualification leads that you are generating. Then you follow steps 2-4 above.

While they watch the video, you direct them to click the button below the video. When they do, they will have to fill out a lead generation form – another hurdle.

Why? Because your marketing systems can be very powerful. You need to make sure you focus on offering your time only to qualified referral prospects.

After they fill out this form, they are then able to book time with you to explore a potential partnership. The following example is from Calendly.com.

These appointments simply pop into your calendar on autopilot. You do a bit of research on that Realtor and then confirm the appointment.

Once you get on the phone with the Realtor, the tables have been turned because the conversation focuses more around what they need to do to work with you. Remember, you have The Irresistible Offer to pitch to them. Every call is an opportunity to generate free leads and deals for you.

Now for our third and last referral partner attraction campaign...

3. Leveraging Listings into Leads

This campaign strategy works to generate mortgage leads who have yet to talk to a lender. You will use your Realtor partners' listings to advertise to people who are interested in real estate but have not yet found the right house.

Full disclaimer: These leads are low-quality and do not convert right away. It's normal to see closing ratios around 1% (as in, 100 leads convert into one deal). Considering your follow-up is completely automated, it takes almost none of your time to execute.

The main reason you run this kind of campaign is to show value to your Realtors and build a database of prospects who are going to buy in the future. The offer for this ad is to get the full details of the listing and find out if the person can qualify to own that specific home and what rate they can expect to pay.

Here is how the campaign works.

Upfront, you ask your Realtor partner to send you their hot listings as soon as they have a link. You create a Lead Campaign with facebook.com/business/ads. (This is a Facebook and Instagram campaign that uses a Facebook lead form to capture the lead directly - no landing page needed.)

Next, you will build a 'carousel' ad to rotate multiple pictures that feature three to five nice images of the home. Your headline is "*Brand New Listing (View Pictures)*."

Your body copy outlines the main features of the home and includes the price. Your call to action says, "*Click the link to get the full details and see all the pictures! To find out how much this home would be for you and what rate you can expect to pay, request a free analysis.*"

Each lead who fills out the form goes into your automatic follow-up system to get pre-qualified.

Now each listing that each of your Realtor partners gets becomes a new lead source for you and you strengthen each of your relationships every time they get a new listing.

There you have it - three incredibly powerful ways to drive deals and new referral partners into your business.

Three Realtor Pain Points

There are three main pain points, or problems, Realtors have that you can use to 'hook' these relationships.

First Pain Point: The first Realtor pain is they're leaving money on the table with their past clients, and they know it. When you talk to a Realtor about database marketing, they always know they could be doing a better job. With just what you have already learned from this book, there are very few who you couldn't help do a better job with their database marketing to make more money.

Second Pain Point: The second pain point is that Realtors pay for leads and then do a terrible job following up because they're busy. When they tell you that they're too busy to work on their leads, or they're too busy to convert those leads, that's another way of saying "*I'm too scared to get rejected when I follow up on leads because the leads are traditionally low quality.*" That is okay because it can be exceptionally profitable if you can convert even 4% or 5% of their online leads. What you have to do is remove the cold-calling and lead-chasing, so they don't have to feel like they're getting rejected. Your offer to do that work for them is a win-win scenario.

Third Pain Point: The third pain point is what Carl calls "rollercoaster income," meaning income is up one month and down the next.

This pain relates to the first two pains (above) because they're not doing a great job networking with their past customers, and they're paying for leads, investing that money upfront, and then not following up on the leads for which they've already paid good money. So, their income is consistently inconsistent. However, you're the rainmaker and the problem-solver - you can solve all these issues for your Realtor partners.

You can go out and generate new deals for them. You can run your own social marketing campaigns to generate leads who want to get pre-qualified, and then pass those over to your Realtor referral partners.

To calculate the potential return on investment from your Realtor referral partners, typically they have (about) two deals per every 100 database contacts. You should be able to convert approximately 4% of their leads into deals (and, as mentioned previously, that ratio will be about 10% when you run your own campaigns). When you can deliver these kinds of results, you have an irresistible offer.

So now you've identified who you want to go out and talk to, you know their pain points and what's going to trigger them to want to work with you. Now let's work that process so you know how to get these 'free' high-quality referrals from their databases.

Getting High-Quality Leads and Referrals

There are a few different ways you can get into a conversation with Realtors about high-quality leads. You might reach out to them over the phone, meet them at a networking event or use social marketing to get them to book an appointment with you. Or they might approach you to co-market or buy their Zillow leads from them.

In whatever way that conversation opens, your goal is to slide into it this question: "*How many times this year have you called your past customers to get referrals?*"

This is a loaded question, especially because your next question is, "*In your experience, how many referrals do you think you could expect if you called four times a year?*"

It will be incredibly rare to hear they're calling their database quarterly. What that means is you are helping them unpack the value they're leaving on the table. Even if they don't express it to you by telling you in that initial conversation, they will be doing the math in their head and it will clearly highlight their pain point.

When you offer to share this script with them (for free) to help them solve that problem, you're a rainmaker and a problem-solver. Share the following message in a voicemail and let them know they can use or modify it to use with their quarterly calls too.

"Hey, [insert Realtor name], your name popped into my head so I thought I would reach out and say thanks again for your business. I've been calling my past database with this message and I'm getting great results. I thought you might want to use it too. I say, "Hi Mr/Mrs Jones, this is your favorite real estate agent Mary. I was just calling to check on you. It's been a fantastic year so far and I hope you're still loving your home. Now, if anything changes,

please feel free to reach out. I'm happy to help. And I just wanted to remind you our business is built on your referrals, so if you know anybody with questions or are looking to buy or sell, simply CC me in an email - my email address is [insert Realtor email]. You can also tag me or my firm on social media or feel free to pass along my number. I'm happy to make sure they get the same amazing experience we had together. Hope you're having a great day and chat soon. Again, this is [Insert Realtor name] at [insert Realtor's company / firm name.]"

At that point, they will think, "*I don't have TIME to do that. I'm not going to sit down and spend two days out of my life to call my past customer database. There's too much pain there. The phone is too heavy.*" And now you have them right where you want them.

Now what do you say to them? *"I would be honored to help you with this. I have the staff and software to make this happen. We will upload your past customers into the software, record a message from you (that sounds like it is just for them but is really sent to everyone) and then broadcast it in one fell swoop. We can do this quarterly and change the message to fit the season. I'm doing it with my database, and I'm seeing great results from it. Can you see how making these connections can result in closing more deals from your past customers? Remember, I'm not asking you for any of your new business. All I want to work with you on is the business I help you generate."*

That's your Big Hook. *"Would you like me to do that for you?"* Because not only are you eliminating their pain point, you're providing the solution and then going further by eliminating all the work in getting the result.

By asking one simple question to unearth a big pain point, and already having a proven solution you've used yourself, you have an absolutely irresistible offer to go out and get the lowest-hanging fruit in their business for them.

Of course, their past customers may call them, regardless of whether you've helped them generate that referral. But what you anchor in the mind of that Realtor referral partner is you're the person who helps get them deals from their past customers. So, when they get a referral from a past customer, they naturally think of you.

When you think about a Realtor's database, what are the highest-quality, easiest-to-close customers? Those referrals who come to you who are referrals that have

---

come to them. Right? The double-referral is the lay-down deal everybody really wants to gain access to – and this is how you can do it.

The best part is it takes very little time to set the whole thing up and then you have this deal flow for as long as you have that relationship.

Now let's talk about other ways to help bring in business for them.

Free Leads from Zillow, Boomtown, Facebook, etc.

This strategy all starts with another simple question. It will help you get the leads your Realtor partner gets from any online source – Zillow, Boomtown, Facebook, etc.

This will be part of the same initial conversation regarding their past customers. Many times, these first two questions are enough to provide substance they find valuable in establishing a relationship with you. Here's your next question. "*What is your conversion rate for your online leads?*"

Boom! This will likely open a can of worms with that agent because most of them say, *"Terrible! Online leads are no good. They take so long to close and they're expensive. I'm paying Zillow X amount of dollars."*

Time for you to ask another loaded question, *"What does your follow-up process look like for those leads?"*

In just that split-second question, you'll hit their second pain point of, *"I'm generating the leads but I'm not getting a result."* They've already told you they aren't converting their online leads. What you've just done is surface the pain point of not having a system for conversions. So, again, they're spending money to acquire those leads without nurturing them properly. Even if they are co-marketing with someone, they likely don't have a follow-up system in place. Most call leads two to three times and then give up.

Your irresistible offer to someone who is buying leads is to help convert those leads for them. Here is your script. *"I have a system that will call, text and email your leads until they cry "uncle!" I know all those phone calls can be daunting. I propose we work some of your older leads from Zillow and Boomtown and any other services you connect* to for leads. We can even help work your Facebook and Instagram leads.

"I'm not asking for your fresh Zillow leads or a co-marketing arrangement with you. You probably have something like that in place already and I don't want to interrupt that relationship. All I ask is you give me your leads that are 60 to 90 days or older and let me work them for you. You've already paid for them. They're not being followed up right now - they're sitting in a desk or a database somewhere. Just give me those leads and let me show you what I can do with them for you."

Your offer is, "Would you like me to do that for you and convert those leads? I'll work your past leads for free. When you see that it works, then I'll work your leads in real-time, but only when I have shown you that this process actually works."

Now imagine getting all those 90+ day old leads from Zillow, Boomtown, Commission Inc., Facebook, whatever their sources are, and putting them into your follow-up system. You're pre-qualifying the deals they've already invested the money for, passing them back and using that success to win the relationship going forward with that real estate referral partner. It's an incredible way to build value, solve a pain point and become a rainmaker for them, all with just one little simple conversation and a system.

The best thing about that is those aged leads actually get better over time! Leads that close in under 30-60 days are the anomaly.

Most of those leads aren't going to convert for 60, 90, 120 days. The money is in the list of leads because people who are looking at houses today still need to go through that whole process of buying that house. Almost all your real estate partners are going to think that a 60-day old Zillow lead is no good.

The reality is a good portion of those leads are just coming into the market and just becoming mature at this point. You get to connect with 30% (or more) of them for free and you get to build value with your real estate referral partner as a result of doing it.

Obviously, this is a powerful strategy. By making this a standard part of every possible appointment you do with one of your real estate referral professionals, all of whom have these pain points in trying to make the online game work, they learn you are the solution to their problem.

The Ultimate Hook

While you're still in the initial conversation with your Realtor referral partners, you can use what we call 'the Ultimate Hook'. This can also happen in a subsequent conversation if you need to prove your system first and establish the relationship.

Either way, you know you want to win their business. You know they're worth on average about six deals a year for your business. You've asked if you can help them with their past customer database and whether you can help them with the leads they've already generated and paid for to make the most of their investment. The third loaded question to ask them is:

"Would it be of value if I could provide or generate pre-qualified leads for you? Would that help you?"

Talk about irresistible, right? Let's talk about how you can do that.

Inquiry Form

Fill out this form, scan and email it to stay in touch, schedule a meeting with Carl and / or Chris to discuss building your business faster and easier with digital campaigns.

Your Name: _____

Business Name: _____

Mobile Phone: _____

Direct Email: _____

Website: _____

What do you want to discuss?

- ☐ **Digital Campaigns:** Personalized marketing strategies.
- ☐ **Referral Systems:** Ways to streamline workflows that yield automated high-quality referrals.
- ☐ **Team Development:** Talk about growing my team.
- ☐ **Business Coaching** with Carl and/or Chris to grow my business.
- ☐ **Have Carl and/or Chris Speak** at my next event.
- ☐ Other: _____

Please Complete the Form, Take a Picture and Email It to:

Carl.White@TheMarketingAnimals.com**.**

How Online Marketing Works

There are three phases of online ads - 1) targeting and getting your ads in front of the right person, 2) the qualifying offer which is the call to action in the advertisements you run and, lastly, 3) the conversion piece you use to convert your leads (this can be a short-form loan application, for example).

We've eliminated opt-in pages from our conversion funnels because that's the lowest threshold in lead generation. What you want to do in the qualifying offer (step number two) is qualify your traffic as being the highest-quality customer. That means you are targeting the right people, giving them an offer through an advertisement that only attracts quality people, having them jump a few hurdles before they can opt-in to show their motivated interest (just like your potential Realtor partners do), and THEN they can give you their name and contact information.

Once all that is complete, the lead moves into step number three – the conversion. Remember, we are talking about automated lead conversion, which means sending them the ringless voicemail, text messages, and emails, then turning that lead into an inbound phone call.

If you miss any one of these steps, your whole marketing funnel can blow up! If you're targeting the wrong people, you're going to get the wrong people through the funnel. If you're not qualifying people properly, you will get 'garbage' leads. If you're not following up with your leads properly, you will have good leads that fall off the back of your funnel because they never reach out to you. You must have all three steps dialed in for your process to work.

Let's focus in-depth on the first two steps; we will consider the third step - automated lead conversion - a bit later.

Doing the Math

What you're doing is finding interested prospects on Facebook and Instagram, then moving them through a process to create customers in your business. Let's walk through the math on how this works so you can have a realistic expectation of what to expect from your marketing campaign(s).

For example, let's assume you are making $2,500 per deal, and that you have a monthly online advertising budget of $1,000. Let's also say you're spending $10 to get each lead. What you're about to learn is a way to get your lead generation costs down to $7, $6 or even $5 each. The better your optimization gets during the optimization phase of this process, the lower your cost per lead and, bonus, the better the quality of your leads.

But let's talk worst-case scenario. Both of us - Carl and Chris - have weathered some pretty hairy situations that cost us more than expected. Now is our chance to use that for your benefit. (At least something positive can come out of our 'unexpected outcomes'.) (Who said the word 'failure"? We don't have those!)

Anyhow, let's show you how to map out the numbers to have a realistic expectation of how online marketing works. Remember, these are different than referrals from Realtors or referrals from your past customers.

When these kinds of leads start with your ads, they have no idea who you are and they're far out on the early edge of the buying cycle. Facebook is identifying them as coming into the market and their interest in getting a mortgage but, most often, they're 90 - 120 days out on actually making that purchase decision (and creating that income check for you).

So, you have to know upfront you're targeting people to bring into your funnel who are 3 – 4 months away from purchase. What you're doing is building an asset in your business that's going to be exceptionally profitable in the future (a pipeline). It's just like investing in the stock market.

In month one, you're going to put in $1,000 for advertising. You're going to need to generate 100 leads at $10 to make that viable and, remember, you will not have any closings from this investment (for now). Yes, you're going to have leads who come through the funnel. And you're going to get better at working these leads. But, basically, you're just going to have those people come through the funnel. At the end of month one, out of 100 leads, you'll probably end up with 5 – 6 high-quality people in your leads list.

That leads into month number two. You spend another $1,000 on ads. You're making an investment and generating another 100 leads. That brings you to 200 leads. You've invested $2,000 in traffic and, again, you've got no closings and no return on your investment. (Your goal isn't to get every lead - your goal is to get the exact *right* leads.)

Next, you're going to get leads from month number one that start to mature and work their way further down your funnel. You're going to get new leads in month number two who you open conversations with, start pre-applications with, and start working down your funnel. But, realistically, nobody shows up in that 60-day window and says, "*Hey, I'm buying a house tomorrow. How fast can you get me approved?*" As much as we'd like to see it happen, it just doesn't.

When you see people talking about it and running ads about that on Facebook, it is not the norm. That is the outlier who comes in through your funnel. Sure, it happens and it's great. There's low-hanging fruit out there - but we don't blow smoke. We want to be crystal-clear in setting your expectations with this strategy.

By the time you get to 90 days, the end of month three, you've invested $3,000 in your online ads and you've got 300 leads in your database. You're still spending $10 a lead. But now, you close your first deal from the system.

This is somebody who came in during month one, got pre-qualified, who you referred to a Realtor, who went out and found a house, made an offer and it was accepted. It was a relatively fast deal. So, you've closed that one deal.

That means, of the $3,000 you've invested in traffic, you are now $500 in the hole on your investment (figuring that your average commission is $2,500). This is where the numbers start to change for you because of the power of compounding. Remember, internet marketing is just as much about math as it is the actual conversion of the people through the funnel.

By the time you get to month four, you invest another $1,000 in ads; that brings your total investment to $4,000 now. You've got 400 leads in your database as a result that are being worked by your automated system. Now you close another two deals from month one and one deal from month two. You're still working all the leads from month three and, again, you've got a small pool of people who came in during month four so you're having conversations with them. You're getting ready to pre-qualify them.

With those three closings, again assuming $2,500 commission per transaction, you have brought in $7,500, minus your $4,000 in advertising costs. Your return is now a positive $3,500.

Now you're at month five so you invest another $1,000 to bring your total investment to $5,000. That gives you 500 leads total in your database that you're working through your automated system. By now, you should have closed six deals total - one from month one, a couple from month two, a deal or two from month three. That brings you to a total of six closed deals on the system, right? (Not six deals in that fifth month - six total out of those five months).

This means you've just crossed the point where you've, essentially, closed a deal per month using your system because you are five months into the system. Again assuming $2,500 in commission per transaction, you're now net positive $10,000.

Now you roll into month number six, where you close four more deals in that month to bring you to a total of 10 closings in six months; your return on your original investment of $6,000 goes to $19,000.

This is how digital marketing works. This is what we call the 'compound effect' and the snowball that happens in your business.

Now, you might think this process seems difficult. And you're right - it is a little difficult, until you know what you're doing.

When you extrapolate these numbers out over a year, and then look at having this investment at a year and a half, and then at two years, while continually putting in that same relatively nominal $1,000 monthly investment upfront, your return continues to compound because your database continues to get larger and larger and larger and you continue to convert business.

By the end of the first year, if you look at just the first six months, the traffic you're generating and the leads you bring in during the first six months of running a program like this, a 4% conversion ratio puts you at roughly 24 deals in a year.

Disclaimer: we are NOT making any income projection statement or guarantees! But if you can see 1,200 leads into your system in a year, and only 24 closings on the back end, many people will say, "*I want to convert a lot more people into deals.*" And that's great! But we urge you to focus on the system / map and the return on the annual investment you've put into the business because that's where the real magic happens. This is the reality of digital marketing.

But here's the thing – when you are using these strategies online, it's like having billboards on the freeway. Even when you're driving at freeway speed, you see these billboards so by the time you've arrived to the next exit, you know what to expect – the business name is familiar to you. That's what happens with these strategies – you become familiar, a social celebrity, so your coffee dates and appointments increase, and prospects "magically" have higher availability to meet with you. There are no more cold calls – only connections based on people feeling like they already know you. And that's going to skyrocket your results beyond basic digital marketing.

We do this in our business every month. We bring in new leads, nurture them to the point where they convert, and we know the average customer is not going to create a return for us for 60 - 90 days. Carl often says you can predict your results in 90 days based on the activities you do today. That is absolutely true for digital marketing.

We go into this strategy knowing the investment we make today is an investment in the future that WILL generate a return (provided you do great follow-up). Even more, our efforts are compounded in terms of results. Digital marketing can be exceptionally profitable. Our intention here is to give you a realistic expectation of what it takes to roll this out for your business.

Your Targeting Blueprint

There are three types of traffic online. There is cold traffic, where you go onto Facebook and say, "*Hey, find me people that are interested in real estate or interested in a mortgage.*" Second, you have warm targets - people who you have in a database somewhere, or you're able to target by creating a lookalike audience on Facebook. (We'll share what a lookalike audience is in a bit.) The warm targets are also your referral partners - people you're working with or know on a regular basis.

Lastly, you have an audience in what we call an 'indoctrination loop', or an 'attraction loop', where you continue to feed them high-value content to 'indoctrinate' them in your business philosophy and approach.

What we're talking about here is very advanced strategy - to put really good mortgage loan content on social media, designed to attract *only* a person who is ready to buy a house right now. Anybody who consumes that content is retargeted with very compelling ads to get on the phone with you and go through the qualification process. People in the indoctrination loop tend to be very high-quality leads, built off the first two audiences.

One of the rookie mistakes that mortgage professionals often make in online marketing, say using Facebook, is to target people who are interested in mortgages and real estate and every interest option they can possibly think of to cram into the Facebook targeting algorithm. They save all those search requirements as one ad set, and then run one ad to all those people. Naturally, they get low-quality leads and lackluster results because they're trying to mash all the targeting options into one audience.

You need to know there's cold traffic, warm traffic, and indoctrinated traffic; each of those people need a different marketing message to move them one step further in your marketing funnel. Let's explore that next.

Traffic Means People

The people who see your ad and then click on it are called 'traffic' in the digital marketing world. The social media channel's algorithm will look at the people who are clicking your ad, then figure out the commonalities between all the people who are clicking on the ad.

From there, Facebook (for example) will show your advertisement to more people on Facebook who look like, or match, the people who have already clicked on your advertisement. The beauty of it is that the algorithm is going to go out and find more ad clickers for your campaigns (people who could be interested in your offer). That's how artificial intelligence (AI) works.

There are two main places online where you can target quality mortgage leads: search marketing and social media marketing.

Google and YouTube control the majority of the traffic in the search space.

Facebook and Instagram control the majority of the traffic in the social media space.

First, we are going to cover how to target quality traffic from Facebook and Instagram, then we will cover Google and YouTube.

Facebook and Instagram Traffic

Depending on the audience, you can target traffic in different ways. There is cold audience targeting, warm audience targeting and leads targeting. Each requires a slightly different approach for best results.

Cold Audience Targeting

This is when you target finding prospects who are unknown to you using the general targeting options available on Facebook. You can target all kinds of different options including user location, age, gender and interests.

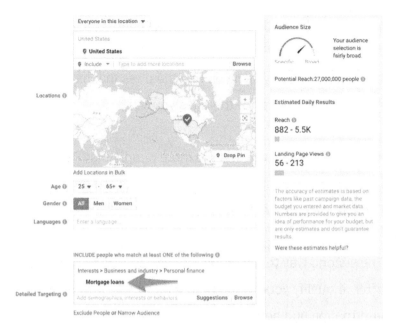

The thing most mortgage professionals (and companies) miss is there are both good and bad quality leads all mixed in when you start advertising to cold traffic. It is just as likely you will get your ad in front of people who cannot qualify for a mortgage as it is you will find your next ideal potential client.

So, you need to train the algorithm inside your specific Facebook ad account as to where the good leads are that you want for your ads.

You do this by testing different ad sets and watching the cost and quality of the leads coming through your marketing funnel. When you find the ones that have a good cost per lead, those are the ones you scale.

The more ads you run and the more people that Facebook is able to watch come through your funnel, the better the Facebook system gets at targeting the right audience.

The second way to get higher quality leads is to use your offer to qualify your traffic before they input their contact information and become a lead. You saw this previously when we used 'hurdles' to show prospects are motivated to take action and pre-qualify themselves with you.

Warm Audience Targeting

You are targeting these audiences differently because, through their behavior, they have expressed interest in you. These audiences include:

- Anyone who clicks your ads or visits one of your landing pages.
- Anyone who watches more than 25% of your marketing videos.

- Your newsletter subscribers.

- Your website visitors.

- Your leads database, like Zillow, Boomtown, CINC leads and other sources.

- Registrants for your workshops or networking events.

- Anyone who has expressed interest in your business but has not yet become a customer.

What do you do with these people? You create specific audiences inside the Audiences section of your Facebook Ads Manager.

What that means is you're going to upload all the people who you're doing business with right now, or have done business with in the past, so you can retarget those people as well as create audiences on Facebook of people who look just like those people. (Get it? 'Lookalike' audience?)

Since these people know you already in some way or are closer to their purchase, they are 'warmer' than your cold audiences. So, you show them ads that have your direct mortgage application offer.

PRO TIP: This is a next-level strategy! If you look at doing only cold targeting, you're playing in the same sandbox as everybody else on Facebook. By using this next-level strategy of lookalike audiences, you're creating your own special audience that only you are advertising to in your market. So, typically speaking, your cost to reach those people is less, it's a more responsive audience, and you'll get a higher-quality lead through this strategy.

Leads Targeting

These audiences for 'leads targeting' have taken you up on your offer for a consultation or submitted an application with you. They should be seeing almost the identical set of ads your past customers and referral partners are seeing. These ads include:

- Past customer testimonials.
- Stories of success with other customers.
- Helpful tips and explainer videos.

The only thing they don't see is a call to action to send referrals.

By simply following these best practices for targeting your audiences, you can launch your campaigns with a competitive edge and generate better results in the same local market.

Now, let's walk through your targeting on Google and YouTube.

Google and YouTube Traffic

In the same way you just learned, you need to handle cold audience targeting, warm audience targeting and leads targeting appropriately to meet them where they are in their current relationship with you and your business.

Cold audience targeting

There are tremendous targeting options when you start advertising with Google Ads. Your main options are to run search ads, local map ads, search network banner ads and ads on YouTube.

Following are what the different ad placements look like.

When you do a search on a search engine, the regular ads normally take up the first four spots (this is on your computer desktop).

When you search on a mobile device, the ads normally show up at the bottom of the search page. The second placement is relatively new and we're seeing exceptional results from it.

GOOGLE ADS + MAP!

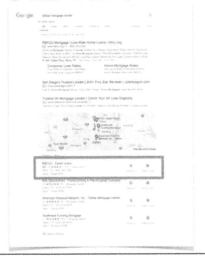

Google now allows you to force your ads into the "3-pack" at the top of the search return. (Until recently, the only way to show up in the top three positions was to use search engine optimization, or SEO.)

If you have a good number of online reviews on your Google My Business profile, please do the 3-pack ad placement as it is exceptionally low-hanging fruit.

The next placement is the content network.

CONTENT NETWORK

Most mortgage professionals have no idea how this works and how powerful this strategy can be in reaching your ideal prospects.

Google serves most of the banner ads you see online. Their content network includes an amazing amount of the national and regional news outlets and websites that are incredibly reputable. You can show your banner ads on those sites for pennies and target the people who are interested in getting approved for a mortgage.

The final placement you can target is YouTube, the second largest search engine in the world. On mobile devices alone, more 18- to 49-year old people watch YouTube during prime time in the United States than they do the top ten prime time shows combined.

The first type of ad is called a pre-roll video, which typically shows up on the video playlist while the person is watching another video.

YouTube Traffic
- Google Ads - Pre-Roll Ads

This placement allows you to show both banner ads and more of your videos with an option to visit and subscribe to your YouTube channel.

The final major ad placement you need to know about is sponsored videos. You can get your video(s) to show up in the suggested videos section alongside videos that are relevant to mortgages. This allows you to target people when they are watching other videos related to mortgage or have recently exhibited purchase behavior.

There are over one billion hours of video watched on YouTube every day - that is an astonishing number. Think about all the financial gurus who have built a reputable brand by giving advice to your clients. People like Suze Orman, Dave Ramsey, etc. You can place your ad on a financial guru's video about credit scores, saving for a down payment, etc. that points to your social call to action. You can target that ad to only people in your local market and you can choose to show it only when they are interested in getting a mortgage!

This is one of those simple twists that can transform your results and create a compound effect that can change your business. Even more, with every network out there, you can take advantage of the most powerful targeting option there is – Retargeting and The $ Loop.

Cliffhanger, anyone??? (Read on... we'll explain!)

Where to Drive Traffic

You are going to drive your traffic to one of two places. Every time you run an ad on YouTube, somebody's going to have the opportunity to click the ad or press the button. If you are retargeting to your past clients or doing any type of

---

brand-building, you want to drive people to your website. This could be the homepage of your website or you can set up a specific offer page; often, it's enough for people to go to your website, see your phone number and call you as a result.

You can also drive people to your Google My Business page; however, if you drive them to your website, you can keep retargeting them (because that's where your retargeting pixel lives). A retargeting pixel is a string of characters that links your social media channel to your website; basically, it's a 'cookie'.

When you are driving cold traffic, using in-market audiences and you're sending them specific types of ads, you want to send those people to your offer page. Your offer page is for them to go through a pre-qualification survey (which could be part of your online app) or through a Chatbot (which simulates human conversation) to find out how much home they can qualify for and what rate they can expect to pay in their mortgage. (We will cover more about the survey and Chatbot later.)

You want to drive cold traffic visitors through a marketing funnel where they give you their information so you can follow up with them via the ringless voicemail, text message and email messages which should convert them into a loan. So, retargeting goes to a brand funnel and new, or cold, traffic goes to an offer-based funnel that's focused on getting their direct response, which qualifies them in working with you.

You want to ask these people, "*How much home are you looking to buy?*", "*Do you have a down payment?*" and "*When are you planning to request your home loan?*" These questions are asked to qualify the lead upfront, so you know what type of lead you're working with and for those who are not a fit to self-select out of your system.

The Secret to High-Quality Leads and Closings

The secret to high-quality leads and closings is to do the opposite of what most people are doing in the industry - make it hard to work with you by using hurdles. You might think that means you'll get opposite results but, instead, you're going to get fantastic leads that come through your funnel. You will not need to chase or cold call these people. You're going to let the system do the work for you.

Rather than making it easy for people to opt-in to your system, making it hard to opt-in is the new pathway to success. Why? Because most people in the industry are giving really low threshold offers, like, "*Hey, if you want a list of upcoming foreclosures in your marketplace, fill out your information.*" Then those advertisers are using lead forms where Facebook will pre-fill in all their information, and all the visitor has to do is tap a button twice.

That strategy was great for creating low-cost per lead results, in the $2-$3 per lead range, but the people who come through those funnels are lower quality. It's just how it works. These are wonderful people – they're just not your people, your best leads.

That's why we take an opposite approach to this process. Our recommendation is to say, "*I'm willing to spend a little more per lead because I want a higher-quality lead to come through my funnel, so I don't waste time working a lead that's going to be difficult or not pan out.*" Your time is your most valuable asset! You need to look at this strategy and make a return just like investing in the stock market.

Your goal is to put in an investment today and, in six months, create a great return on that investment. It's very difficult to do that with low-quality leads. You need the highest-quality leads to come through your funnel.

To make that happen, you want potential customers to demonstrate their readiness to work with you by giving them things to do after they've clicked on your ad. When the person jumps through hoops, they're serious – people simply won't do it unless they really want it.

The first hoop your potential customer has to jump through is reading the ad and responding to it. Rather than writing ads that give a flashy offer, your ads are repellent to unqualified, superficially interested people. You want to repel people with low credit. You want to repel people who are just going to waste your time and not be qualified. You want to attract only people who have a down payment, who have good credit, and who are in the market for closing a loan.

Next, you want that person to watch a video in which you share valuable information about how you work with your clients. From there, you might ask qualifying questions and, when the answers they give match your criteria for an ideal client, they are directed to share their contact information so you can schedule a personal call with them.

By the time the person goes through a three- or four-part process, answering your pre-qualification questions, they are invested in working with you and you have a high-quality lead.

Online Marketing 101

So far, you now have systems to generate more deals from your past customers and referral partners. Now we can add the marketing systems that will drive new leads and customers to grow your business faster.

As you already know, the three core components to a successful online marketing funnel are traffic, the offer and the automated conversion follow-up systems.

THE FUNDAMENTALS

TRAFFIC SOURCES — THE OFFER — THE CONVERSION

Google YouTube

Current Income   The $ Loop   **Future Income**

Think of your funnel like a table with three legs – if you come up short on any one of them, you won't be sitting comfortably, meaning your campaign will not perform.

Traffic – We covered the subject of traffic; however, to refresh, traffic is the art of getting your message in front of the right borrowers with the right credit profile at the right time. The amazing thing about online advertising is the longer you run your campaigns, the better-quality traffic you generate.

The Offer - The second step to generating high-quality leads is making sure what you offer to the marketplace, in exchange for their information, qualifies people as viable leads and gives you permission to follow up with them. We talked about the Irresistible Offer previously; ideally, every offer you make to any audience or visitor is irresistible.

The Conversion – Without conversion, great traffic is meaningless. Online leads are skeptical - with good reason! Most companies generating leads online do not do a good job of following up and delivering on their promise. The campaigns you are learning use ringless voicemail, text and email messaging to create an exceptional bond and convert cold leads into warm applications automatically.

Closing Loans from All 4 Online Platforms

We have three campaigns to help you close loans from Facebook, Instagram, Google and YouTube as follows.

1. The $ Loop: Retargeting people who know you.

2. The Chatbot: Direct mortgage leads from an automated pre-approval tool.

3. The Survey Siphon: Direct mortgage leads from gamified lead funnels.

We will go into these campaigns later. For now, before you get started building your campaigns, there is some crucial information you need to understand about marketing online to close deals. If you skip these fundamentals, you will end up wasting money on low-quality leads that never become closed loans.

You are going to learn how to get your ads in front of the right people, how to qualify them with the right offer and then how to build an automated follow up system that converts your leads into inbound apps on autopilot. It's

---

called a marketing system and it can be exceptionally profitable for your business.

Each of the core drivers of your business should have automated systems so that they can grow at scale and without you having to continually invest your time.

Retargeting Made Simple

Retargeting is the powerhouse tool most professionals, including mortgage loan professionals, running their own advertising budgets online completely miss. It's exceptionally important to do retargeting as part of your online campaigns.

What you have likely learned up until now is what we call 'the old funnel' where you go into Facebook, do the cold targeting options, show an ad, present an offer (like a lead form, list of foreclosures or a listing), then try and drive people to your application. That's what most people are doing right now.

However, costs for that style of advertising are going up dramatically. Simply going after cold traffic with a blunt offer that's not social is now being penalized because

Facebook wants their members to have a quality experience with valuable content and engagement. If you have a relevance score of less than six inside your Facebook Advertising Account, you're going to have a hard (expensive) time in the future when it comes to your campaigns. You have to make sure people are having a good process and responding well to your Facebook ads.

The best way to set yourself up for success is to understand the reality of how marketing works today and then play by those rules.

We are all blasted with information and advertising all day long. That means that, even when a consumer likes what they see about your business or are personally referred, they will forget about you. By simply following up with continued advertising and reminding your audience of how you are the best option to help them with getting their mortgage, you will win more business.

The Big Four major online platforms drive more than 80% of online traffic. When you follow up well on all of those leads, you have an exceptional market advantage. As mentioned previously, we call it Omni Channel Marketing. This tactic alone has decreased our cost per lead by more than 50% and increased the closing ratio on our leads by more than 10%. Here's how it works.

No matter what platform your traffic or leads are coming from, you place a retargeting pixel that you get from both Google and Facebook on those visitors. When you do that, you have simple campaigns active on all the networks that target only your warm traffic.

Again, you then show them testimonials from past clients. educational videos and calls to action designed to drive traffic into your landing pages, opt-in forms and website.

What does this mean in practical terms? While your competition struggles with cold calling and chasing leads day in and day out, your automatic advertising system attracts your buyers to you when they are ready to take action on their mortgage loan. It's the perfect set-up for you to step in and help them.

Now, let's move on to how you attract quality leads from your properly targeted traffic.

The Offer

We already covered what an Irresistible Offer looks like for your Realtor referral partners. In online marketing, there are four key pillars in making an offer; these pillars are the same for all four social channels (Facebook, Instagram, Google, YouTube). The only thing that changes is the way you deliver the ad (image vs. video).

Doing the work to create a good offer just one time can create an asset for you and your business that you can leverage into leads and deals for years.

This exercise is going to walk you through creating the offer that will attract leads from your online advertising. Then we'll cover the other three campaigns we just mentioned to generate stellar high-quality leads.

Four Principles of Online Advertising

The four principles of online advertising are market, message, medium and timing.

The Market – The Market is comprised of people who are in-market and actually need your services. They have the credit criteria you are looking for and your product meets their needs. For example, a mortgage lender might look for a home buyer who is actively shopping for a home, who has a down payment, good credit and a 'now need' to find a new home. Or, an insurance professional would likely want to attract someone who is in immediate need of initial or expanding coverage - new parents who are relocating and shopping for a home in a new city.

The Message – The message is you speaking directly to their needs and actually helping them through your advertising. That means you are not pitching them on your great rates, service and 'vanilla' messaging that everyone else says... instead, this is a very specific message which speaks to the core of what your customer wants right at the time when they want it.

Here's an example of a message directed to a first-time home buyer looking for a mortgage.

"Did you know that the first offer you get for your mortgage is often FAR WORSE than the offer you can actually get? It's one of the reasons that banks post such exceptional profits each year. Most buyers just never do their research.

Don't let it be you. I will take any offer you get and help analyze it for free. If it's a good deal you can rest assured knowing that you did your research. If it's not, I can help you make sure you get the right mortgage for your needs AND negotiate the lowest rate for you. Book a free mortgage strategy call today by clicking this link or calling 1-800-XXX-XXXX."

The Medium – The medium is about putting the right message in front of the right market in the right channel, where they are actually hanging out. It means positioning yourself where they are already looking. A decade ago, the medium was the local newspaper's classified section and the Yellow Pages. Today the right medium is Facebook, Instagram, Google and YouTube.

The Timing - The fourth element to crafting a successful offer is timing. You must be able to give the right offer to the right person at the right time. The good news is Facebook, Instagram, Google and YouTube do all the hard work for you and give you the data you need to time your message properly – and it's free.

You can literally put your advertising message in front of an interested prospect just days after they have started exhibiting the purchase behavior that lets these social platforms know the person is looking to buy what you have to offer.

The timing might just be the easiest part. However, you need to dial in the market, the medium and the message to make the most of timing for the best conversions.

Shortcuts in Creating Your Offer

The Market

Your market is comprised of the people in your specific location – do not try to build a nationwide campaign first. It's better to build a campaign that's successful within a local market before you start to scale.

The second part to finding your market match is working backwards from the specific product you're going to sell and then niching out to the specific people who need that product.

For example, when it comes to a first-time home buyer, there's a typical age demographic, an area demographic,

---

and a specific psychographic of that person who is looking for a home.

There are also more subtle things you can identify about a first-time home buyer. Are they buying a condo or a house? Are they getting a gifted down payment from their parents or going through a government program? Will they have other friends who have already bought a home, or will they be the first in their group of friends to be purchasing this home?

On the surface, these seem like minute details. But, when you start giving the message to your market, it allows you to choose the right images. It allows you to write the copy that will actually call out to that specific person.

Your marketing message, regardless of the medium, must deliver a message that is so clear it stops your perfect prospect in their tracks. Think of your ads as personal 'notes' to just one specific person. Why? Because your ideal customer lead should see that message in their newsfeed and feel it was tailored right for them, like one of their friends had written the message directly to them. When you nail your ideal customer profile this deeply and accurately in your campaigns, you will win every time.

When you're writing your ads, think about the exact person you want to bring through your funnel, and write ad copy as though you're writing an email specifically to them. The more specific, the more you call them out. This is almost like your elevator pitch on social media. You go out, give that offer to the right person, and the Facebook algorithm will do the rest of the work.

Remember, you're going to retarget and build audiences off people who get to the end of the funnel. The ads at the very beginning need to repel as many people as possible so your system gets more accurate and profitable over time.

Naturally, there is a challenge to this. You've probably realized that you can "niche down" to at least 10 different types of first-time home buyers – each of whom needs unique ad copy and ad sets. So, start with your perfect customer, launch your first campaign and grow as you need or want more leads.

The Medium

The shortcuts to the medium are very simple in both Facebook and Instagram. Remember, you need separate images and copy for Facebook and Instagram – you can't use the same image in both channels and maximize the effectiveness of your campaigns. Why? Because Facebook has an older demographic while Instagram has a younger demographic.

On Facebook, you have a lot of copy options while on Instagram your image or video needs to do most of the explaining for you.

Three Message Frameworks

Effective messaging has three core frameworks - pain, pleasure, humor – which are enabled by right timing.

The Pain Message

As human beings, we are fundamentally hardwired to avoid pain. Mortgages, insurance, complex finances and legalities all are associated with transactions that people deem painful. Why? It can be scary to get a mortgage, buy a home, contact a lawyer and shop for insurance.

So, when a new lead approaches you from online advertising, it is normal for them to have their guard up and feel like they're going to be taken advantage of by a potential provider. Just remember it's not about you personally.

Giving people a sense of empowerment and education through your advertising makes you irresistibly attractive when they are in the purchase mode. You become the pathway away from a painful and scary situation.

What's the number one pain point or problem your ideal customer is trying to solve? That becomes your core message for that ideal potential customer audience.

Once you create a post that alleviates the pain for that person, the lead will be pre-framed to work with you because of a simple, targeted advertisement.

The Pleasure Message Framework

The second framework for creating your advertisements is pleasure, meaning that you are bringing people toward an experience to enhance their lives while also solving their problem. Testimonials, success stories and stories of transformation are examples of pleasure messaging.

In your ad, you can show how someone just like them met a mortgage professional (you) and learned about something they didn't know (like a government grant or gifted down payment), which solved a problem, and resulted in a fun and empowering experience. By telling the story, you are showing them you have already helped people just like them escape the pain of a stressful process and they had fun doing it.

This type of advertisement provides a level of security through the advertisement and makes a big difference.

The Humor Message

The third message framework is humor. People use social media to stay connected and entertain themselves. When you put a boring mortgage rate ad below the latest viral video, you are not differentiating yourself and you will likely lose the person's interest (and their business).

However, humor allows you to position yourself differently and cut through the noise to reach your prospect. For example, you could say something about how completing a mortgage application for your first home is about as exciting as watching paint dry - which is why you offer a quick application process. "*In just 10 minutes, you can be pre-approved and on to shopping for your new home with confidence in what you can afford. You will know the rate you can expect to pay so you can get your new home and start painting!*" :+)

Timing as An Enabler

The enabler for your best and most targeted offer is timing, which is taken care of by the social networks. Simply use the traffic targeting tips you learned previously in this book - choose people who are interested in mortgages or new homes in your local market. Remember it takes time to train the social channel's algorithm on who your perfect customer is but, once you have the basics in place, you can see fairly quickly who is in your ideal audience.

Now, you understand why most online leads are low-quality and why so many companies struggle to convert online leads into customers.

Two Ways of Making an Offer

There are two ways to approach making an offer.

The first way to make an offer is to create something "flashy" that will attract as many leads as possible.

The second way is to create something of VALUE that will generate far fewer leads but bring in more qualified prospects.

Both can be very powerful ways to attract and convert business, but you must understand which offer method you are using and determine the outcome you want before you launch it.

The ad framework you learned previously in this book promotes brand new listings for your realtor referral partners. That is a flashy ad campaign, where you can generate many leads for very low cost – between $2 - $5 for each lead.

Now, these leads are low-quality in that most may never end up purchasing real estate or needing a mortgage and/or are at the very beginning of the home buying process.

Most of the quality leads who will end up purchasing a home will not do so in the first three months of becoming a lead and, because most professionals do not follow-up well, those leads never turn into closed loans. It's normal to close 1% or less from these kinds of ads.

However, if you understand that the purpose of the offer is to initiate referral relationships with Realtors as referral partners who will send you all their other leads and referrals for free, then this campaign can be exceptionally profitable.

Think about attracting just three or four new Realtor partners for an investment of just $5 per day for each new listing ad to maintain value in that relationship. Even if it was a total flop and you only got one referral a YEAR, at a commission of $2,000, you would make a significant profit. And you will likely do far better than just one referral every twelve months.

How? Simply put, you need to know the market you are going after and then choose the right campaign and use the right offer to hit your performance targets.

Three Loan Campaign Strategies

As promised, here are the three loan campaigns you can use to close more loans on social channels.

1. The $ Loop (Retargeting)

2. The Chatbot: Direct mortgage leads from an automated pre-approval tool.

3. The Survey Siphon: Direct mortgage leads from gamified lead funnels.

Let's explore each in the following pages.

Campaign 1: The $ Loop

Here is where technical strategy gets even better, or, as Chris would say 'fun'.

Social media is notorious for generating low-quality leads. However, you can feed the information from the high-quality leads (based on credit score and other factors you determine) back into the algorithm and tell Facebook and

Google to ignore the low-quality leads. This is putting retargeting on steroids! We call it The $ Loop.

THE $ LOOP

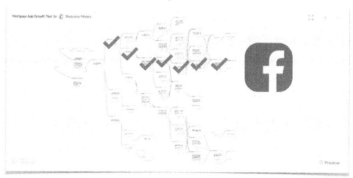

When a lead you want to work with comes through your marketing funnel, tell the platform(s) to go find more of those people – and the platform(s) will do just that.

You see, when you are using the general targeting options on the platforms, they are targeting ALL the credit and finance leads - good and not-so-good.

Think of your audiences as a big pie. Some slices of the pie are perfect, full of high-quality borrowers looking to make a move right away.

THE STRATEGY

Other slices of the pie are garbage and have people who won't qualify for a loan, no matter how bad they want to get a loan for a new home. (Disclaimer: These are not necessarily bad traffic – just not the best traffic for you. They would be perfect for a credit repair service – but you want high-quality, ready-to-go borrower leads.)

Our strategy allows you to force the algorithms to only serve up the best slices of the pie and leave the other slices for your competitors.

The longer you run your ads, the better your targeting gets and the better your entire marketing system will perform. Although it can take months for your system to refine itself, it eventually gets to the point where you can outperform your local competitors by leaps and bounds.

NOTE: Yes, this is a little technical; however, once you do this process even one time, this is an asset you own and you're now working with the social media channel's algorithm in this little blue ocean of uncontested market space that nobody else can access. It's all about slotting different ad sets based on budget and then, over time, testing your budget across each of your ad sets to see which ones generate quality leads so you can scale them, and which generate very low-quality leads so you can shut them off.

Remember Re-Targeting

Remember, every new lead who fills out your survey is going to go into an automatic follow-up system to turn them into an inbound inquiry when they are ready to talk with you. Those leads will go into an Omni Channel Marketing and Retargeting system, so they see ads from you all over the internet.

These ads will show them education and helpful mortgage tips, testimonials, stories of success and calls to take action and complete your application process.

Since you will be a social media 'celebrity', familiar and recognizable, your follow-up messages will convert better, and the closing ratio will increase on the leads from whom you take applications.

Campaign 2: The Chatbot

When you get to the level in your business where you have a budget to invest money into advertising to generate direct customers, going direct to market for generating mortgage loans is the best pathway.

Remember, you must create value and then promote that value through your online advertising. When your goal is to convert online traffic into customers, it is important to shift your focus from generating a lot of leads to generating high-quality leads. Your time is your most valuable asset; the more time you spend talking to unqualified borrowers is the sacrifice in time you could be using to attract new referral partners (or chilling on the beach).

So, your offer is designed to qualify your good leads and repel the low-quality leads before they get the chance to input their contact information and become a lead.

We recommend using chatbots to talk about borrowing to get your leads to qualify themselves to you. Naturally, you are targeting who sees this offer which, over time, will improve the credit profile of your leads as the platform learns who you are most interested in as a lead.

What Is A Chatbot?

Since we have only referenced it quickly so far, a chatbot is the secret weapon we are most excited about right now because we are seeing the highest quality leads come through the process. The caveat is you must be willing to engage in Facebook Messenger to make this process work.

A chatbot is an automated conversation that happens on Facebook Messenger. You run an ad, someone clicks on it, and your software starts a communication exchange, or a conversation, with that person. They know it's automated. People know it's a bot but now people believe it's easier to work with a bot to get the information they want because they are afraid of a salesperson. Self-service is a trend in automated marketing. (Convenience is a powerful tool.)

So, the bot guides them through the exact same application process as a survey funnel (which we will cover next). The chatbot sends the prospect messages inside Facebook Messenger, and they choose the options to answer those messages and questions inside Messenger.

These leads are much higher quality because they have self-selected through the process, they have gained information and they are ready to have a conversation.

When you search Google for 'chatbot price', you will see there are companies charging a minimum of $30,000 for a simple bot. A top-of-the-line premium bot can cost as much as $150,000. The good news is you can use a service called ManyChat for just about $10 a month and you can build your own bot.

Following is a sample chatbot conversation a prospect might experience, in case you haven't seen one before.

"I noticed you have interest in mortgage loans right now. Is this a good time to chat?"

The person can click yes, no or "I have a question." If yes, the bot will continue with the conversation. If not, the bot will ask them to schedule a good time. If they click on "I have a question", the button takes them directly to your phone number where they can just tap a button and call your office.

If they click yes... "*Okay great! Let's get started. Tell me what you are looking to do. Purchase a home, refinance, renewal (if in Canada)?*" (You have previously configured these options, so they are customized to the type of lead you want for your business.)

If the person clicks on 'purchase a home', the bot says, "*Awesome! That's our specialty. What's your price range? Up to $400,000, $400,000-$750,000, or $750,000-$1,000,000.*" So that person shares key budget information.

Basically, the bot is asking pre-qualification questions to determine whether this is a good lead for you. If they are not a lead who matches your criteria, then they will be encouraged to pursue other options and will not be added to your marketing funnel.

"*Have you been pre-approved for a mortgage in that price range? Yes or no.*"

From there, you might want to ask about their credit score, timeframe, etc. The idea is that the chatbot handles the pre-qualification process automatically.

The Chatbot Sequence

Start by running your ads to be placed in front of the different traffic types who are interested in 'mortgage' on all four platforms: Facebook, Instagram, Google and YouTube.

The first step in qualifying the lead starts with the copy of the ad text or the video. It speaks only to a person who has good credit and who wants to apply for a mortgage right away. Once they click the ad, they are taken to the next step in qualifying themselves to you. You want your leads to come to you vs. you chasing them down.

This next step means asking advanced questions that only qualified leads will take the time to answer. The following questions are examples of the types of questions you want your chatbot to ask at this point.

- What are you looking to do? Purchase? Refinance? Get a Reverse Mortgage? Take advantage of your VA benefits?

- What is the loan amount you are looking for? (Be sure to offer three ranges.)
- Do you have a down payment?
- What do you think your credit score is?
- How soon are you looking to make a move?
- Are you working with a Realtor?

You don't ask for their contact information until they answer all the questions you need to know upfront. Once they've answered those questions, and their answers show they are pre-qualified for the type of client you want to work with, get their name, email and phone number so you can follow up personally.

Instinct would tell you that this would decrease the number of people who come through your marketing process and/or it would increase your cost per lead. But the exact opposite is true!

Why? Because when you go from being very broad and generic with your ad copy to ad copy that speaks specifically and only to people who are interested and in the market for a mortgage, you will get a better caliber person through your marketing funnel. We have found we get a conversion rate of 10% - 15%. Then, by adding chatbots (and surveys), we got even better-quality leads with 35% - 45% of the leads completing the entire survey. That is a 4x boost on the same ad spend for a better lead who is interested in mortgages vs. just real estate.

Campaign 3: The Survey Siphon

The Survey Siphon is basically the same process as the Chatbot strategy but in a sequential online survey. You want to ask your prospects the same questions you need to know to complete a short-form application. When you keep the questions to three or less on a page at a time, it is less overwhelming for the person to answer the questions.

You have probably taken online surveys yourself, where you can see a status or progress bar about how far you have gotten into the survey (10%, 40%, etc.). That plays into our subconscious mind because we naturally want to be at 100% completion. The human mind does not like open loops – so the inclination will be for your prospect to complete the survey, or short-form application.

Once you receive it, you can determine whether this is a pre-qualified customer for you and act accordingly.

Two Bonus Types of Campaigns

In case you are an overachiever, you should know there are other types of campaigns. We will not cover these in detail in this book, but we did want to point out that the world of online advertising has many, many options for you to consider in growing your business. Here are just two additional campaigns you might want to consider in your marketing plan.

Traffic-Based Campaign: Every different consideration or objective you select in your campaigns will work differently. Facebook, for example, is going to show your ad to different types of people. In running your first Facebook campaign, you want to run a traffic-based campaign because that means Facebook is going to try to drive traffic (people) to your offer. That's a fantastic way to start optimizing your results.

Once you have traffic going to your offer, and you can see what's converting and have a baseline for your projected conversion rate, you can say to yourself, "*I'm driving traffic into this chatbot (or survey) campaign. I'm getting leads at $5 a piece or $7 a piece. Whatever it is, I'm happy with that. I'm willing to spend $X amount on traffic to get X number* *of leads."* You can then go back in and create a conversion-based campaign.

Conversion-Based Campaign: A conversion-based campaign will watch the people who are not clicking on the ad but are actually filling out their information on the landing page or the short-form survey or whatever mechanism it is you're using to convert the lookie-loos into leads. Then Facebook will start to use its algorithm (it's AI, or artificial intelligence) to go find people who are like your leads (the ones who have taken action on your ad) - not just the traffic who is looking at your ad. A conversion campaign will get you a better customer in the end and produce a higher-quality lead through your funnel than a traffic campaign.

Now a quick caveat to that - conversion campaigns can only work if you're giving Facebook enough data so that Facebook can identify what your best lead looks like in their system.

If you're not generating ten or more leads a day, which is what we found Facebook needs to figure out who our high-quality leads are, stay with a traffic-based campaign. If you're scaling and getting more than ten leads a day, choose a conversion-based campaign because you will get a better and higher-quality lead to go through your automated marketing funnel.

Close More Loans Using Follow-Up Automation

You now have two of the three core marketing system components built. You know who your ideal audiences are, you're targeting them properly and you're giving them the right offer which prequalifies them as a high-quality lead and potential client. Now comes the part where most professionals totally drop the ball - follow up.

When you get a new lead in your business, how diligent are you with your follow up process?

Do you have a secret file with old leads who could have been a deal, but you were too busy to work them at the time?

Of course you do! Everyone does.

Check out these shocking sales statistics...

SALES STATISTICS

48% OF SALES PEOPLE NEVER FOLLOW UP WITH A PROSPECT

25% OF SALES PEOPLE MAKE A SECOND CONTACT AND STOP

12% OF SALES PEOPLE ONLY MAKE THREE CONTACTS AND STOP

ONLY 10% OF SALES PEOPLE MAKE MORE THAN THREE CONTACTS

2% OF SALES ARE MADE ON THE FIRST CONTACT

3% OF SALES ARE MADE ON THE SECOND CONTACT

5% OF SALES ARE MADE ON THE THIRD CONTACT

10% OF SALES ARE MADE ON THE FOURTH CONTACT

80% OF SALES ARE MADE ON THE FIFTH TO TWELFTH CONTACT

Source: National Sales Executive Association

The idea is it takes an average of approximately eight contact touchpoints to convert a prospect into a customer. And more than 80% of sales professionals stop short of this goal.

If you review the actual sales statistics in this study, 48% of salespeople never follow up with a prospect. If you recall, there are Realtors who are paying for leads who fit into that category. That's why it's so powerful for you to make the Irresistible Offer - "*Hey, I'm not looking to interrupt a relationship you already have in place. I am just looking to work with you on the deals that I help generate. Doesn't that seem fair?"*

Interestingly, only 12% of salespeople make three contacts and then even they stop. That means only 10% of salespeople make more than three contacts.

As Carl teaches, what generates results is the total opposite of what people are doing. Research shows that 80% of sales are made between the fifth and twelfth contact. We all know it takes people an average of seven times to see your marketing message before they respond to it. That number is going up because we're so bombarded by advertisements and getting numb to all those inputs. But it makes sense that people choosing a mortgage lender will need to hear from you multiple times in order to feel comfortable picking up the phone. And yet, most mortgage professionals stop following up well before having an opportunity to win that business.

Getting into the nitty-gritty, that means if your follow-up process stops after just two attempts (one call and one text), you are missing 88% of the deals in your pipeline. We know this to be true from our research.

In analyzing over 11,000 leads we previously generated for our social media marketing clients, we learned the following information.

- It took an average of sending 5.1 messages before a lead responded (including ringless voicemail, text and email).

- We had a 42% response rate by following up 15 times with a prospect. This is compared to less than 20% if we followed up only five times.

The Best Time To Follow Up!

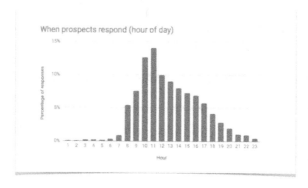

Time of day and the day of the week matters in terms of people responding to your outreach messages. You might not think so but between 10 am and 12 pm is surprisingly good.

Even so, the reality is it's getting harder to get people to open an email. We find a 30% open rate on emails is a pretty fantastic result. That number means your database is very responsive and, if you're getting that off new leads, you're doing something right. It means you've got great subject lines, great copy and a great connection with your audience.

Typically, your average email marketing will get a 15% open rate, meaning just 15% of the people who got your email opened it. Typically, post-transaction email open rates will drop to around 5% from people who have gotten a mortgage because they're done with the transaction.

What this means is they've processed their loan and don't feel they need to engage in any of that communication anymore. So those post-transaction numbers shrink rapidly. If you look at actual click-through rates, when you get 15% of people opening your messages, you're doing great.

After the recipient opens your message, they have to respond or engage with it, which means to call you, email you back or click through the link you've sent them in order to take action and engage with you. If you can get a 5% click-through rate, you are crushing it.

There are industry giants who don't achieve even close to that 5%. From a commerce-based perspective, 3.5% on a click-through rate is considered tremendous. If you're getting a 1.5% click-through rate on your messages, that's about typical. Again, when we measure post-transaction, less than 1% of the people who opened the email will actually click on the link or engage with anything in the email.

Putting that into perspective, that means for every 100 leads you generate in your system, if your primary communication channel with them is the internet marketing method and you're only sending them email to get them to respond, you'll get about 30 opens. And then, of the people who actually click in the email, you will get one and a half responses, which is a 1.5% response rate from 100 leads.

That's not nearly good enough for us to make this system work. We know that compounding our communication through multiple channels creates a more significant effect. In this case, 1+1 can equal 5 – that's the compounding effect in action.

What we do is continue to email people because it does get a response. But we also text message them, call them on the phone and, via our automated system, send ringless voicemails.

The response rates are remarkable. Typically, we'll see a 1% to 5% response rate via email. We get about 15% of our responses through text and then we get about 25% of our responses from our voicemail messages. Some of those people are calling back direct, while others listen to the voicemail and then text us back.

The big takeaway here?

THE MONEY IS IN THE FOLLOW UP.

Here's the big advantage of the marketing systems you are learning in this book. You are going to get to a point where you cannot keep up with all the leads and opportunities in your pipeline. Generate just 50 leads in a month and, very quickly, all the names start to blend together. So, you must have a system to capture the money in your database and marketing system.

In any case, we can attribute these responses back to the original voicemails. You can see the difference in the response rates you can get by applying the compound effect based on the leads you're already generating. If you've got 100 leads that come into your system, simply by compounding (adding in ringless voicemail and text messages), your open rate goes to 95% because everybody listens to their voicemail and most people will open all their text messages.

That open rate number goes even higher when we add in Facebook Messenger. You take it from 1.5 responses to 40 responses just by adding in two more communication channels and not really having to mess around with getting super fancy with the messaging or anything like that.

Our first core lesson here then is, just by adding in those other two channels, you get this compound effect in your marketing where all of it works even better.

The Sequencing

Now, how often should you be messaging your leads to get them to convert?

The key is to understand you are going to have four different types of people who are entering your funnel and you need to have messaging that is going to convert all four types.

1. Buying Phase - These people want to talk to you right now. They have found the right home and are ready to get approved. (This will be the fewest number of leads in your funnel.)

2. In-Market Phase - These are the people who will respond to the offer right away but need the five touches to get them to chat with you. They are actively shopping for homes or need to refinance but have not hit their trigger point.

3. Research Phase - These are the leads who will take weeks or months to convert. They are keeping an eye on interest rates, market trends and neighborhoods for the right home. They are not ready to convert and will not be

for at least a couple of months. This segment of your leads presents a tremendous opportunity to build the relationship, generate referrals from these leads and help when they are ready.

4. Awareness Phase - These are the tire-kickers and rate-shoppers who may never be ready to purchase. They will respond at all different points in your marketing funnel. Whenever they do, qualify them as fast as you can and unsubscribe them immediately if they are not a fit.

Compound Communication Systems

In the system you are learning here, there are nine contact points – meaning nine outreaches in the first three days. Here's why. A lead will be the most responsive in the first 24 hours. We have done lots of testing and we find that a lead is most responsive within the first 10 minutes. If you can get that lead on the phone in the first 10 minutes, you will have a much better conversion ratio than trying to call them even a couple hours or days later. Our system is to have the ringless voicemail drop within the first two minutes because we know that gets the best response.

When somebody is on their phone, they're engaging in that mortgage offer. They submit the information. Your likelihood of converting that lead goes up exponentially when you communicate with them right away. Now you may pick them up on the second or third or fourth message but, by sending that initial voicemail right away, you have the highest likelihood of converting that lead because you've conveyed your professionalism. You've given them your contact information and you've done it in a way where you've made it convenient for them to reach back out when they are available.

We're going to talk scripting and processing to get into the nuts and bolts. But, basically, at the third contact point, we've got a 21% response rate, meaning 21% of the leads are responding to the third message. Then, 20% of those leads are responding at the fourth message. After that, the statistics trail off. But if you're leaving your leads after the first two follow-ups, you (and your Realtors) are missing out on 88% of the deals that you're generating in your advertising simply by not following up correctly.

It is vital to put these long-term systems in place. We can no longer rely on ourselves in order to do this follow-up.

When you see a lead come in and know that lead, and every single lead you generate, is getting a very professional, very well-thought out, structured process that gives you a reliable result, it's a game-changer. The best part is you don't have to depend on yourself to do it! You just set it up once and it works for you forever.

Imagine the lead sources you've engaged with previously. What would have happened to your income, and your business, if you had had 45% - 50% of the leads respond back asking for a conversation? That's what this whole system does for you. It sends the ringless voicemail, the text message, and the email in a system - at the best time on the best days so that you know you're going to get the highest response rate from your leads.

Here is the process of how to schedule your follow ups to get these kinds of results. On day one, when a lead opts in to your marketing system, a ringless voicemail goes out after two minutes. Then, 10 minutes after the lead comes in, a text message goes out. Next, 15 minutes after the lead has opted in, an email goes out.

That may seem aggressive but you're simply offering to give them the information they've asked for with professional, consistent follow up. As soon as the lead responds to any of the messages, the system shuts off. At that point, that lead should be entered into your CRM (customer relationship management) system.

Oh – and the reason you don't want to put these leads straight into your CRM is because many will not be responsive. There is no need to clutter your CRM with pointless leads.

Continuing on... let's say they didn't respond and now you're on day two. At 10:00 a.m., which is when people tend to respond best, send them another ringless voicemail. At noon, they receive a text message. If you still haven't heard back, at 2:00 p.m., send a follow up email.

Remember, this person has requested information through one of your campaigns. They've requested to find out how much home they can afford and what rate they can expect to pay. You are simply responding to their request, ready to give them that information, and being professional with your follow up.

At this point, you are just two days into your marketing relationship and you've already reached the basic five points of contact needed to get the majority of leads to respond.

If the person still hasn't responded on day three, another ringless voicemail goes out at 10:00 a.m., then text message at 12:15 p.m. and then an email at 4:00 p.m. Those are spaced out in terms of timing, so it doesn't seem robotic. Day one, day two, day three.
This completes the first three days of follow up. At this point, we typically see 25% to 30% of the leads having responded.

If you've had no response by day three, cool off and wait until day six. Then send another text message and another email. Now, all these messages are very similar because you know they're either not reading them, or the timing just isn't right and it's okay to give that person the same offer multiple times. The offer is good, you're just waiting to get them at the right time that's going to convert them.

Knowing you have covered the eight touches it takes to convert the hot leads, you take a break so we can keep a strong bond with the leads who are going to convert in the future.

If by day thirteen, when there is still no response, the person gets another text and another email. On day 30, that person gets another text message at 4:00 p.m.

On day 39, at 10:00 a.m., they get a voicemail. On day 50, they get an email at 10:00 a.m. On day 55, they get another text message. Lastly, on day 60, they get the final voicemail. After that, drop them into a sequence which communicates with them once a month with a friendly check-in message - "*Hey, if you have any questions, feel free to reach out.*"

At this point, you've essentially taken that lead and done everything possible to convert them and done it in the most professional manner possible. You've taken it all the way to the 60-day mark - and you are going to continue beyond that.

Often, the leads who have been in the marketing system for 60 days are better quality than when they first became a lead because they are further along the buying process and are finally ready to get qualified.

So, there you have it... an automated conversion machine that turns all your leads into inbound phone calls and appointment requests.

The Benefit of Aged Leads

Remember when we mentioned the timing on aged leads you are working with your Realtor referral partners? When you drop their leads into this system, those leads have already reached 30 – 60 days in the cycle. That means the timing is much more 'now' for them to take action - that's why "aged" leads convert so well.

Keep in mind this works for both new leads that you're bringing into the system that you're generating from Facebook or Instagram or Google, and it also works for all your Realtor leads as well.

One more thing – when these aged leads come in, you want to work with them hot and heavy with the whole system vs. dripping out a monthly email. This is about cultivating awareness and relationship and providing a way for these people to get the information they want and, typically, they are just getting ready by the time you start working them. The results can be quite shocking because their responsiveness can be much higher than you might predict in advance.

The Messaging for Your CRM

The messaging that goes into your CRM system should be customized to your business, especially if you are running any type of special funnel. If you're doing refinance funnels, or you're doing VA or FHA, or if you've got a specific loan type that you're looking to do, like reverse mortgages, you've got to make sure that you're giving at least some type of customization to the person who is coming through the funnel to get their response.

Remember, you've used targeting on Facebook to do a very good job of getting into these little, tiny slivers of traffic that are very high quality. You're showing ads to those people while repelling the people with low credit to eliminate negative leads and only be attractive to the people who are interested in and capable of getting qualified right now. Your goal is to provide value while pre-qualifying them for a loan.

With all the effort it took to identify them, you don't just let them opt-in – you ask them to jump a few hurdles. *"How much home are you looking to buy? Do you have a down payment? What's your credit score? Have you ever been previously bankrupt?"* As the leads are going through those stages, you're qualifying them by showing them messages like, "*If you have a minimum credit score of this, this won't work for you.*" And you're removing them from the funnel. You're doing everything you possibly can to get a quality person to the end of this funnel. That's why this system gets such a great response.

Each of these systems build on the others. If you're just going to take this follow-up system and dump a bunch of leads that are a year old into it, it's not going to work. If you're going to run generic Facebook leads and give an offer that says, "*I've got a list of foreclosure homes that I can get you hot deals on real estate*," those are garbage leads. They're not going to convert.

Everything you're doing upfront culminates in the best-quality lead, with them responding to your messages, then getting on the phone with you without you having to do any of the follow-up, or chasing, which is what happens in many marketing initiatives.

Example: The Automated Conversion System

Here is an example of the first initial voicemail. Keep in mind this voicemail script is an easy message that leverages the other elements of your already-established marketing system. You are being cool with people vs. badgering them with a sales process. Just be cool, be nice, and people will be attracted to you because they're the right people.

"*Hey, It's Chris Johnstone. I got your request to find out how much you qualify for and what rate you can expect to negotiate in today's market. I have that information for you. Simply give me a call back at this number or just shoot me a text. I'll send you a message here in a couple of minutes*

---

so that you have my information. I'm looking forward to chatting with you, and hope you're having a great day."

Super simple. "*You have requested something from me, I have it, and I would like to give it to you.*" You never, ever get people angry at you for saying, *"I'm doing what you asked me to do."*

Now here's the text message that follows up. It says, "*Hey, [NAME], I have the information that you requested about your mortgage amount and what rate you can expect to pay in today's market. Let me know when a good time is to chat so I can get this information over to you.*" Then it's got your name, your email address, and your phone number. And remember, by sending this text message, you have just inserted yourself into the contact book of that person's cell phone.

If they come through on your chatbot funnel, you're not in their Facebook Messenger but you are in their phone contacts via the text message(s). So, when that person has questions about mortgages, they will actually go back, find you, and message you back because you've sent these messages.

After the text message, there's a simple email that says, "*Hey, [NAME], just a friendly follow-up to the messages I sent this morning. I got your request to find out how much you qualify for and what rate you can expect to pay. Simply let me know when a good time is to chat, and we can go over everything. You can also reach me direct at the number below.*"

Those are your scripts for your voicemail, text message, and email. And you continue to send variations of that because, again, you're not hammering people with weird marketing messages or rate updates or anything they're not interested in – you're simply replying back to them with the information they wanted. As you saw, this process is going to get people to call you. So, what do you say to them when you get them on the phone?

The Scripts

This is the phone script that is going to get the application. Remember, this person wants to talk to you, so it's not like you're getting on the phone with them and they're worried that it's a trick or a trap or anything. They've been in communication with you and they have replied back to you. You are not cold calling them. They're calling you or they're texting you.

There are basically five steps to this process. From a very high level, all you're doing is positioning yourself as a consultant. So, when somebody calls and says, "*I want to know how much I qualify for. What's your rate?*", your response should be, "*Great! I've got just a couple of clarifying questions on the information you put into the form. I'm going to pull it up here on the computer in just a second, but I don't have it on front of me.*"

"*Remind me again what price range you were looking to get qualified in?*" They tell you. "*Okay, great.*" At this point, you're qualifying the lead to determine whether you want to stay on the phone with them and continue to convert them or let them go.

"*That's a great price range to be in - do you know what down payment you have saved for a home?*" Then they tell you – "*I have a down payment*" or "*I don't have a down payment.*" "*Okay, great. And what's your credit look like? You guys feel like you're going to have any credit problems that I'm going to come across when we pull your credit, or is everything looking pretty good over there?*"

"*We've got a couple of bumps in our credit.*" "*Okay, well, no problem. What I can also do is once we find out where you*" *are, I can give you a couple of tips on how to get your credit score up, and that will help you with your rates and all that good stuff. But don't worry, I'll walk you through that when the time comes."*

"So, are you both working right now? Is it you and a spouse? Tell me a little bit about that." You're just walking them through the application process.

As you're there collecting this information, you're keeping track of it. You're typing it into an application form, but simply getting the super-easy information upfront to qualify the lead. This is the short form application stuff you're doing up front.

Next you need to qualify the intent of these people. S,o you find out... they're looking at a good-priced home, they have a down payment, or they're at least going to fit within one of the products that you offer in order to get them into a home. They've either got decent credit or they've got income, and it looks like you've got a deal that you're going to be able to package that you're going to be able to work.

Then you ask them the intent question.

"*So, this is great. It looks like we'd be able to move forward on this. So how soon are you guys looking to make a move?*" Pretty simple. "*Oh hey, we're just interested. We're not going to do anything for a year.*" "*Okay, well there's not really a whole lot of point in me pulling your credit right now because it's just going to show as an inquiry. And if you're not going to do anything for a year, call me back 90 days before you're ready. Meanwhile, I'll share good information monthly to help you be as prepared as possible – no worries.*"

Again, you're simply qualifying people through step one and step two of the lead process. When you get them through both steps and you know you can help them, you have to pre-qualify the rest of the information before you ask the question that's going to make them want to bail on the phone. You do that by saying, "*okay, I can help you and we're almost done here. I just need a little bit more information so that I can pull your credit and give you the actual numbers over the phone here. What's your social security number?*"

You get the social security number right up front. You've done a little qualification upfront on price, down payment, credit, income. You need to make sure they actually want to do something right now. You tell them that you can help them and that they're almost done... the process is in motion. And then you ask the hardest question possible, because you don't want to go through any more of the application and get to the end only for them to say, "*I'm not really interested in giving my social security number over the phone,*" or voice some other their objection.

You ask for that difficult information right upfront as soon as you can possibly get to it. You take the social security number and then, oddly enough, it binds them to your phone call. At that point, they need and want to finish the application process because you've got what many consider to be the most crucial piece of information in order to submit that application and pull the credit report.

Your actual script might be a little different — these are examples we've found work reasonably well. At the end of the call, once you've got all the details, you give them the prescription. "*Here's what's going to happen next...*" Then you just walk them through the next part in the process and let them know what they need to do next.

All this can take just 15 - 20 minutes, but it needs to be done over the phone. If there was one piece of advice we could give about working online applications, take the app over the phone! It can be tempting to say you can help them and shoot over an email with the details, but you will lose 80% of your leads if you let them go off the phone. You need to do the hard work for them. And when we say hard work, we mean typing. You simply have to fill out the boxes.

Keep in mind 80% of your customers are going to open your emails on their phone. As soon as they click a link and see a long-form loan application pop up on their phone, their thumbs cramp up and they will think, *"there's no way I am going to go through this B.S."*

So, if you want to take the app from that person, you have to put a system or process in place in order to take the app over the phone and make it as easy as possible for them.

If you get the objection of "*I just want the rate*," deflect. Let them know it's not really up to you to give the rate over the phone until the process is at the proper point. You have likely experienced this in the past when someone has said, "*hold on – my computer is working slow today.*"

The strategy behind the deflect is to keep the client on the phone and build rapport while gathering information and telling them about the process. Just continue asking those qualifying questions over the phone. As soon as that person is on the phone with you from this lead generation system, they are in an application. You're either qualifying them or you're submitting an application and you're just moving them down each step in the process.

Your Database

We've already covered quite a bit on your database but there is still a little more to be thorough about it. We talked about having your database go into a system, then sending a ringless voicemail every three months for follow-up. However, our recommendation is that, once you're in this system, you take every new 'past' customer you have and follow this process.

As soon as your deal closes, have somebody in the processing department (or do it yourself) enter that person into a thank you sequence. They've done business with you, you've collected the money - now it's time to make sure you have a fantastic long-term relationship with that client. The new term for this kind of marketing is 'customer marketing', where you retain the relationship to upsell your services in the future.

So, your person goes into this nurture sequence, and it sends them a ringless voicemail. The voicemail goes like this: "*Hey, it's Chris Johnstone. I just wanted to reach out again and say thank you for your business. It's just wonderful to know you, and if you have any questions, please feel free to reach out. As I mentioned when we first started working together, our business is built on your referrals. So, the next time you run into someone looking to buy, sell, or refinance, please send them an email with my contact information or tag us on social media. I would really, really appreciate it. And I'm going to follow up with you. I'm sending over an email with a link to our Google profile. If you could take a minute and help me out with a review, I'd really appreciate it. Thanks again so much, congratulations, and we'll talk soon.*"

It's a nice touch after the transaction — it feels like the final bow. You're letting them know you're in the business of referrals and that you're going to be asking them for that rating and their review.

Remember, very early on in the buying process, you set the expectation that you would ask them for their rating, review and referrals. If you haven't done that, it's okay to ask for it after the transaction as well.

Here is the follow-up email that goes out after that request. The subject line is their name. The email says, "*Hope all's well. Congratulations again on closing your loan. Would you be able to take a couple of minutes and do me a quick favor? Head on over to our Google My Business page and leave us a five-star review and leave a quick post on what it was like to work with us. Here's the link that you need,*" and then the link to the Google My Business page goes in there.

"*Here are some quick samples to help save you some time.*" And that's where you post your best past customer reviews from real customers. Just paste them in there so they can see what other people have done.

Underneath that, say, "*Of course you can just put it in your own words. Thanks again, and if you have any questions, feel free to reach out at any time.*" And then your signature goes on the bottom with all your contact information so people can reach out to you.

This works. Take it and implement it in your business. We want you to get great results from it.

Deal Targets

To circle back to where we started, here is a baseline on how to hit your deal target and the number of deals that you need in order to hit your goal. Your business might be slightly different than this but, as a baseline, this is a great place to start.

For every 100 past clients you have in your past customer database, you should be doing about 24 deals per year. That's two referrals a month you're closing from your past customer database. That means if you have 200 past customers in your database, you should be doing about 48 deals per year.

For each referral partner you sign up to help work their leads through your business, you should average about six deals per year. That will flex a bit depending on whether they are whales, tuna or tilapia but it should average out to be about one deal every other month.

For every 100 leads you generate, you should have about a 4% conversion ratio, which means about 36 deals a year. Remember, that conversion ratio number is a rolling total because you're not going to get to that 4% conversion ratio until you hit month four, month five, month six. The leads you generate in month one will likely not convert until month four, five or six; the leads you generate in month six will be converting at about a year. The first year you start generating leads, provided you're doing 100 leads a month, you should see about 36 deals a year; from there, your results will compound.

This is the baseline – the number of deals from past customers, referral partners and leads you generate as a total. This gives you the information you need to map out your specific income plan for how many loans you need to close in the year and how to get there.

Now that you know on an annual basis how many deals you need to get to achieve your income target, you need to look at the three funnels, or levers, you have available to leverage in your business. These are the small hinges that swing the big door and are where you're going to get your volume from over the course of the year. You want to map out this big blueprint so that, every day, you know which of these levers (funnels) you're focusing on and what results you need to get from each one to achieve your goal.

To summarize, with what you've learned here, for every 100 clients you have in your past database of closed clients you should close 24 transactions (through refinances, referrals and them moving.) For every agent you have that sends you six transactions or more per year, you should close half a loan a month. So, if you have 12 agents, you should close at least six loans a month from them. And, finally, your 'direct to market' funnel should generate 100 leads each month, to net you 36 deals (over the course of a year).

Note: All of this is on top of your current business that you're already doing.

With your past customers, in order to get the most deals, you need to send lump mail once a month. You want to send voicemails through the automated system to touch base with them at least once each quarter, and then re-target them with ads on social media so you can generate those referrals.

If you have eight real estate partners, that should generate roughly your 48 deals a year. Your market may vary – you might get fewer deals from each Realtor. As long as you're measuring your results, you'll know what activities you need to do and how many real estate referral partners you want to get in your business.

Let's say you feel you already have funnel one working in cultivating your past customers and you don't want to mess around with marketing, so you focus only on referral partners. You could do that, as long as the numbers show you are making progress toward your goal. That's the beauty of working this system – you decide what funnels (levers) you want to use to build your business.

As long as you know the goal, and how many deals it takes to get there, you can determine the daily activities you need to do in your business. You might think you don't want to work with referral partners – in that case, you would be looking at combining funnel one (past customers) and funnel three (marketing) because you know that 1,200 leads in a year - converted at 4% - should put you around the 36-deal mark. To double that number, double your ad spend and double the amount of leads you drive through your funnel. See how fun this gets?

Once you've got this large-scale plan to grow your business, it's very easy to see whether you're on track every month because you know exactly what you're going to do in the year and what that boils down to on a monthly and weekly basis.

to do in the year and what that boils down to on a monthly and weekly basis.

Summary and Next Steps

We are lucky to be in the mortgage business in that we get to help people achieve one of the greatest dreams in many people's lives - to own a home through our service. But sometimes the pace of business makes it hard to remember the impact we're having in the lives of our clients.

Everything you do is, naturally, something you believe will help you be happier or more fulfilled. Helping more people by closing more loans is, ideally, part of that formula. Now you have the recipe for success to create fresh momentum in your business with leading-edge digital and social media strategies, tools and tactics.

The key here is to work smarter, not harder. Use technology as your servant; let it do the heavy lifting of generating leads for your business. Delegate anything someone else can do to make the most of your time so you can focus on what really matters – the relationships you have with your customers, Realtors and other referral partners. (It goes without saying that family and loved ones are your first priority.)

In today's digital business environment, technology cannot do everything your business needs but the loan officers who don't understand and leverage technology will get left behind. Now is the time to make the most of what we shared here – they can quite literally be the pivot point that changes your business (and your life) going forward.

So, follow through on what you've learned here. Of course, we have your back! We encourage you to drop us a message and let us know what you've learned and how things are working for you in your business. Just visit the website at MortgageMarketingAnimals.com, listen to a podcast at LoanOfficerFreedom.com or attend one of our live training events, found at MasterMindRetreats.com to help you make a bigger difference with your buyers and agents through your business.

Carl and Chris

P.S.: If anything in this book brought up questions for you, please share them on our wall at: Facebook.com/MortgageMarketingAnimals – we'd love to know! (Who knows? You may inspire our next book!) :+)

While you're at it, please make sure you post a comment or a video about how much you what you just learned here in this book, ok? Your thoughts could be what inspires somebody else to reach beyond their comfort zone and learn something new to help them grow their business.

The Deal Desk

An Awesome Private Facebook Community That Gives You An Underwriting Resource

Loan Officer Deal Desk

Carl White   Chris Johnstone

The Loan Officer Deal Desk is a place where you can ask underwriting questions when you want an unbiased, educated answer from an actual underwriter.

For instance, if your underwriting is giving a condition you think is not necessary or you need help persuading your underwriter with factual information to help you get that deal closed, then ask away here. You will get a friendly, honest and non-judgmental answer from an actual underwriter so you can take that information to your underwriter and (perhaps) get your deal closed.

We encourage members to give opinions and help each other out with guidelines and suggestions.

Also, thanks so much for inviting your loan officer friends to the Deal Desk community. The more members, the better the resource is for you and the rest of this loan officer community.

You can join the Loan Officer Deal Desk here:

facebook.com/groups/loanofficerdealdesk/

Free Social Marketing Priorities Call

A Powerhouse 1:1 Strategy Call to Identify First Steps for Your Social Media and Google Ad Campaigns

During this free call, we will help you map out a profitable marketing plan that will get you your perfect customers.

If you want to explore help implementing the plan, we can discuss that too. Our team automatically turns 40+% of digitally generated leads into INBOUND phone calls and text messages looking to get approved with you.

However, this is a no-obligation call – our only intention is you leave this call with a clear path to closing more deals through online ad campaigns.

Book a one-on-one marketing strategy session with our team here:

LoanOfficerAds.com/call

The Freedom Club

The Most Powerful Group of Loan Officers in the World to Help You Get Better Clients, Close More Deals and Enhance Your Income

If you're a loan officer or Branch Manager closing eight loans a month or more, then The Freedom Club is for you. As a member, you'll receive all the awesome benefits of Mortgage Marketing Animals.

In addition, you will have access to our full library of scripts for every occasion; loan checklists, systems and processes; job descriptions and ads; tracking sheets for leads, prospects, closings, and conversion rates; employee manuals; advanced loan-getting strategies and more.

Mastermind retreats every 90-120 days with other top-producing members are also included. Most importantly, you will receive personalized, one-on-one accountability coaching every two weeks. Here a plan will be designed specifically around you, your team, your market and your goals for the future.

Want a sneak peek at what it means to be in The Freedom Club? Check it out here:

FreedomClubApplication.com

If you have any questions, just give us a call at **(727) 787-2275.**

The Mortgage Marketing Animals Connected

A Membership Group of Loan Officers Sharing Unbelievably Effective Marketing Strategies

We are a Mastermind Group of like-minded Loan Officers from across the country who research, share and implement an incredible collection of unbelievably effective marketing strategies.

We believe success breeds success and that we are at our best when we as a group are helping others to succeed.

We believe our collective success will far exceed our individual successes.

We believe success is dynamic. It does not stand still. Each of us is constantly becoming either more or less successful.

On its own, an ember cools and the heat it produces dies away. But, as part of a collection of other burning embers, the heat builds and provides warmth for those around it.

This is a members' only group - if you are not already a member, you can learn more here:

LoanOfficerStrategyCall.com

Be A Guest on the Podcast

Twice each month, Carl brings you the best and brightest in personal interviews to discover the keys to success that are working in the field. This podcast is dedicated to inspiring loan officers to take the best of what they know to help them create the business results and lifestyle they really want.

Carl's style is casual, down-to-earth and practical. He empowers listeners while entertaining them and sharing tools, stories and strategies that can accelerate their mortgage loan business results.

Check out the podcast here:
LoanOfficerFreedom.com/

And if you would like to be considered for a guest spot on the show, just call our office at **(727) 787-2275** – we'd love to share your success strategies!

About Chris Johnstone

Chris Johnstone is the of President Connection Inc.

Chris' career started early because his dad is a mortgage broker in Canada and brought Chris into the business.

Unfortunately, Chris and his dad learned that mortgages were not his forte – Chris is not the greatest at paperwork. But advertising... well, Chris immediately fell in love with the ability to write an ad, elicit a response, and then meet a person as a result of that process.

So, the two of them got started running then-Google AdWords for real estate leads. They were generating real estate leads and passing them to the Realtors who would then send them their mortgage business. It was a beautiful thing.

Over the last eleven years, he has gone from being a young entrepreneur running a lifestyle business to now being a ridiculously happy married man with two beautiful children.

Today, Chris has the joy of being responsible for running a corporation with 15 incredible staff (and growing) thousands of customers and a real purpose of helping mortgage professionals profit from online marketing.

Essentially, his company leverages Google, YouTube, Facebook, Instagram, Artificial Intelligence and Follow-Up Automation to create a reliable stream of inbound leads and referrals.

Chris can be reached at:
Email: info@connectionincorporated.com
Phone: (855) 432-3990
Website: ConnectionIncorporated.com
Facebook: facebook.com/connectionincorporated/

About Carl White

I am a husband, and a father to three wonderful young adults. My family and I enjoy boating, camping, and I am passionate about traveling the country on my Harley Davidson while masterminding with the top thought leaders in the world.

On the business side of things, I am the Founder/ Chief Strategist of The Mortgage Marketing Animals and the host of the #1 Podcast for loan officers in America.

I first began my venture into the mortgage business as a loan officer in October of 1999. Within eight months of opening the doors at Family First Mortgage, I became the top-producing branch out of approximately 336 branches nationwide. I also began to train fellow loan officers in my "paint by numbers" approach. This technique helped the LO's retain more closings while working less hours in a week. Five years later, I opened my own mortgage business called Time Mortgage.

Who I Help:
I help loan officers to implement proven marketing strategies I have personally used in my own career and had great success with, measured by hundreds of

---

thousands of dollars in revenue each and every month. While I make no income claims for you (of course), it is my belief I may be able to help you increase yours.

How I Help:
I show specific step-by-step instructions on how to drastically increase your monthly loan production and income while working only 32 hours per week. I do this by teaching loan officers to hyper-focus their efforts, and to stop doing wasteful activities they are currently doing that are not producing measurable results. By following the strategies I provide, my clients are able to regain the freedom to do the things they want to do. Worrying about when and where the next deal will come from is no longer a concern.

Specialties:
Strategizing | Marketing | Advising | Speaking
Video Blogging | Marketing Seminars | Marketing Webinars
Generating Leads | Social Media Marketing | Video Marketing

Carl can be reached at:
Email: carl.white@TheMarketingAnimals.com
Phone: 727-787-2275
Website: MortgageMarketingAnimals.com/
Facebook: Facebook.com/MortgageMarketingAnimals
LinkedIn: LinkedIn.com/in/MarketingAnimals
Podcast: LoanOfficerFreedom.com/
Instagram: Instagram.com/mortgagemarketinganimals/

Made in the USA
Columbia, SC
30 June 2019